THE MOST INCREDIBLE OLYMPIC STORIES OF ALL TIME FOR YOUNG READERS

TRUE INSPIRATIONAL TALES ABOUT PERSEVERANCE AND COURAGE TO INSPIRE YOUNG SPORTS LOVERS

JORDAN ANDERS

CONTENTS

Introduction   7

1. MICHAEL PHELPS   13
   Michael's Story   14
   Michael Phelps Fun Facts   16
   Things to Think About   17
   Up Next   17

2. SIMONE BILES   19
   Simone's Story   19
   Simone Biles Fun Facts   23
   Things to Think About   23
   Up Next   24

3. USAIN BOLT   27
   Usain's Story   27
   Usain Bolt Fun Facts   30
   Things to Think About   31
   Up Next   31

4. SHAUN WHITE   35
   Shaun's Story   35
   Shaun White Fun Facts   38
   Things to Think About   39
   Up Next   39

5. APRIL ROSS & ALIX KLINEMAN   41
   April's Story   42
   Alix's Story   43
   April Ross and Alix Klineman Fun Facts   44

Things to Think About   45
Up Next   45

6. JESSE OWENS   47
Jesse's Story   47
Jesse Owens Fun Facts   50
Things to Think About   50
Up Next   51

7. NATHAN CHEN   53
Nathan's Story   53
Nathan Chen Fun Facts   56
Things to Think About   57
Up Next   57

8. KATIE LEDECKY   59
Katie's Story   59
Katie Ledecky Fun Facts   63
Things to Think About   63
Up Next   63

9. NADIA COMANECI   65
Nadia's Story   66
Nadia Comaneci Fun Facts   68
Things to Think About   69
Up Next   69

10. CARL LEWIS   71
Carl's Story   71
Carl Lewis Fun Facts   74
Things to Think About   74
Up Next   74

11. KATARINA WITT   81
Katarina's Story   81
Katarina Witt Fun Facts   84

Things to Think About   84
Up Next   85

12. CHLOE KIM   87
Chloe's Story   87
Chloe Kim Fun Facts   90
Things to Think About   90
Up Next   91

13. MUHAMMAD ALI   93
Muhammad's Story   93
Muhammad Ali Fun Facts   97
Things to Think About   98
Up Next   98

14. PAAVO NURMI   101
Paavo's Story   101
Paavo Nurmi Fun Facts   103
Things to Think About   104
Up Next   104

15. ERIC HEIDEN   107
Eric's Story   107
Eric Heiden Fun Facts   110
Things to Think About   110
Up Next   110

16. BONNIE BLAIR   113
Bonnie's Story   113
Bonnie Blair Fun Facts   116
Things to Think About   116
Up Next   117

17. YUNA KIM   119
Yuna's Story   119
Yuna Kim Fun Facts   122

Things to Think About   123
Up Next   123

18. WILMA RUDOLPH   125
Wilma's Story   125
Wilma Rudolph Fun Facts   129
Things to Think About   129
Up Next   129

19. MARIT BJØRGEN   131
Marit's Story   131
Marit Bjørgen Fun Facts   134
Things to Think About   135
Up Next   135

20. LAURYN WILLIAMS   137
Lauryn's Story   137
Lauryn Williams Fun Facts   140
Things to Think About   141
To Sum Things Up   141

Conclusion   145

References   149

INTRODUCTION

Imagine watching Usain Bolt dart across the finish line, leaving everyone else in the dust, or seeing Simone Biles' radiant smile as she celebrates her gold medal with Aly Raisman.

These moments, and many others, make the Olympics so thrilling and unforgettable. The Olympics are more than just games; they're performances on the global stage that celebrate our humanity, showing off the skills of athletes from all over the world and celebrating their determination and sportsmanship.

The Olympic Games, which first started in Ancient Greece, have had the amazing ability to bring people from diverse backgrounds together in peaceful competition. They remind us of the power of dreams, the importance of perseverance, and the joy of achieving something extraordinary in life. We all have a chance at winning a gold medal in life. Even if sports aren't your thing, there are plenty of other areas to achieve in and bask in the glory like a true Olympian!

There have been some pretty big changes from the ancient world to the modern spectacles we see today, but the Olympics have stood true as an international symbol of hope, unity, and competitive spirit.

The history of the Olympic Games spans over 2,000 years, starting from the ancient games in Greece held in honor of Zeus and continuing with their revival in the modern era by Baron Pierre de Coubertin in 1896.

The games have evolved over time, including a bunch of important changes such as the introduction of women in the 1900 Paris Games and the development of the Paralympic Games for those with physical and mental disabilities. Each branch of the Olympics' big olive tree continues to promote values of mutual understanding, peace, and respect among nations.

The Olympics are filled with moments that capture the world's imagination. For instance, Simone Manuel's historic win in the 100 m freestyle at the 2016 Rio Olympics made her the first black swimmer to win an individual event. Her emotional reaction and the pride she felt were shared by millions around the globe.

Michael Phelps' intense focus during his races, especially his famous #PhelpsFace, showed the dedication and mental toughness required to become the most decorated Olympian of all time despite being diagnosed with ADHD.

Another unforgettable moment was when Simone Biles, after winning gold in the all-around gymnastics competition, invited her teammate Aly Raisman up onto the podium to celebrate together. This act of camaraderie and support exemplifies the spirit of the Olympics, where athletes compete fiercely but also support and uplift one another.

The Fiji men's rugby team's victory in 2016 brought home the first-ever gold medal for their nation, creating a wave of joy and pride across the small island country. Similarly, Monica Puig's gold in tennis was a first for Puerto Rico, showing how the Olympics can bring monumental achievements to smaller nations and inspire countless young athletes.

The unifying power of the Olympic Games goes beyond individual victories and the number of medals a country has won. The Games bring together athletes from all over the world, competing under a single set of rules and demonstrating their skills in a spirit of mutual respect and understanding. The Olympics have a rich history of promoting peace and solidarity as seen in the tradition of the Olympic Truce, which dates back to ancient Greece and continues to be honored today.

These days, Thomas Bach, the President of the International Olympic Committee, emphasizes the importance of solidarity, not just as a concept of non-discrimination but as an active practice of helping, sharing, and caring for one another. This spirit is at the core of the Olympics and is reflected in the actions of athletes and organizers who strive to make the Games a force for good in the world.

The Tokyo 2020 Games, despite being held under unprecedented circumstances due to the global pandemic, demonstrated how the Olympic spirit never goes away even in the face of global challenges. Athletes from all different backgrounds still came together to compete, showing that even in the face of adversity, the values of the Olympics endure.

In this book, you'll learn the true stories of 20 Olympians who have shown incredible perseverance, courage, and resilience both on and off the field. Each chapter will take you on a tour through the lives of these extraordinary athletes, highlighting the challenges they faced, the obstacles they overcame, and the victories they achieved.

Get ready to dive into the stories of legends like Michael Phelps, who swam his way into history with a record-breaking number of medals, and Simone Biles, who flipped her way to gymnastics greatness.

You'll learn the quicksilver secrets of Usain Bolt, the fastest man alive, and Shaun White, who dominated the snowboarding world. Each story is packed with unique challenges and incredible triumphs that will leave you motivated and excited.

As you read these stories, you'll find that these Olympians started just like you—with dreams and challenges. They faced setbacks, doubts, and failures but never gave up. Let their journeys inspire you to dream big, work hard, and never lose hope. Reflect on your own dreams and think about how you can apply the qualities of these incredible athletes to your life.

So, open your heart and mind as you dive into these stories. Get ready to be inspired, entertained, and motivated. Whether you love sports or just enjoy a good real-life success story, this book is for you. The tales of perseverance and courage you'll find here are all inspirational, and some of them might even help you chase your own dreams with all your might.

As you turn the page, prepare to dive into the pool and swim alongside Michael Phelps, the word-champion swimmer and most decorated Olympian of all time. Get ready to be amazed by his dedication and passion for swimming. So, put your goggles on already, and let's dive in!

Chapter 1

MICHAEL PHELPS

> 66 *I wouldn't say anything is impossible. I think that everything is possible as long as you put your mind to it and put the work and time into it.*
>
> –MICHAEL PHELPS

Imagine diving into a pool with dreams that go as deep as the darkest spot in the ocean. For Michael Phelps, deep dreams of Olympic glory were with him from a young age. He wasn't just interested in winning races though—he wanted to break boundaries and shatter records!

Michael's path to Olympic greatness is one for the history books—built on his dedication to training, the support he received from his family and coaches, and his desire to stay competitive in a big pool of global talent. Michael has shown an impressive level of dedication to his sport and managed to turn his struggles into strengths, setting a new standard for what Olympic athletes can achieve.

Michael's story isn't just about his physical power as a swimmer; it's also really about the mental fortitude he showed throughout his career. He shattered records and collected an astonishing 28 Olympic medals, including 23 golds (The Editors of Encyclopedia Britannica, 2018), making him the Olympic athlete with the highest medal count of all time. His journey to greatness was marked by highs and lows, including a temporary retirement after the 2012 London Olympic Games and a triumphant return to the pool in 2014.

MICHAEL'S STORY

Born in Baltimore, Maryland, Michael began swimming at age 7. It was more than just a hobby for him; it became his sanctuary and a way to channel his boundless energy. Diagnosed with ADHD, he struggled with hyperactivity and faced learning difficulties at school, but swimming provided him with a focus and a purpose. It helped him channel his boundless energy into something productive and provided a structure in his life. Under the guidance of Coach Bob Bowman, Michael dedicated countless hours to training, honing his skills, and refining his underwater technique.

Michael often felt set apart from his peers due to his learning difficulties. All the other kids seemed to be treated differently by the teachers; sometimes the teachers were really mean to him, and he didn't know why. A really important thing happened one day when a mean old teacher told young Michael that he would never amount to anything, a statement that could have discouraged him but instead fueled his determination.

Michael became dedicated to the idea of proving his teacher wrong. He knew deep down inside that if he practiced really hard at swimming, it could lead to something big one day. Swimming became a coping mechanism, giving him a place to focus his energy and a sense of purpose. He was sad that the teachers were mean to him, but he put all that energy into developing disciplined and rigorous training routines.

Under the guidance of Coach Bob Bowman, Phelps's commitment to the sport grew even deeper. As he got older, he trained harder and harder, swimming up to 80,000 meters per week (*Michael Phelps: The Training Regimen of the Most Decorated Swimmer in Olympic History*, n.d.) once he'd reached his prime, in addition to weightlifting and intense interval training.

Michael's relentless work ethic paid off as he began to break records and gain international recognition. The discipline of his intensive training regimen provided him with the stability he needed to manage his ADHD effectively.

Phelps's accomplishments as an Olympian are legendary. His career included groundbreaking performances on the international stage, such as when he won eight gold medals at the 2008 Beijing Olympics, a feat that set a new standard.

After the 2012 London Olympic Games, Phelps announced his retirement, only to make a comeback two years later in 2014. He returned to compete in the 2016 Rio de Janeiro Olympic Games, where he was America's flag bearer and added several more gold medals to his collection. This marked his fifth overall Olympic appearance, a record for an American male swimmer.

After he decided to retire for good, Phelps faced significant mental health challenges, including anxiety and depression. He first experienced post-Olympic depression after the 2004 Athens Games, and it recurred after the Beijing Olympics in 2008.

In 2014, Michael began to understand and address his mental health struggles more deeply. He sought help and started speaking openly about his experiences, aiming to break the stigma surrounding mental health issues.

These struggles have shaped his legacy beyond the pool. He has become a vocal advocate for mental health, using his platform to raise awareness and support for those facing similar issues.

Today, Michael encourages others to seek help and not to be afraid to speak about their own mental health, showing them that if they embrace their struggles, they can find ways to cope.

Michael's legacy extends to charity efforts and advocacy, and he frequently speaks about the role of mental health in sports as well as the impact sports can have on personal development. Michael's Story shows us that by proving people wrong and by embracing our uniqueness, we can go far. He also shows us that we shouldn't be afraid to speak up about our feelings and mental health concerns— that we should be strong advocates for ourselves.

Michael's story teaches us the power of sticking to our goals, no matter how tough things get. He faced many challenges along the way, including learning difficulties and setbacks in his swimming career. But he never gave up! His dedication paid off when he became the most decorated Olympian of all time. Michael's story shows us that with perseverance and hard work, we can achieve incredible things too.

Just like Michael Phelps, we should all embrace what makes us unique. Michael's ADHD and his long arms and strong legs helped him become a great swimmer, but it was his determination and unique way of thinking that truly set him apart. Just like him, we all have special qualities that make us who we are. By embracing and celebrating our differences, we can turn them into great things. So, whether you're great at swimming, soccer, or baseball, remember that your uniqueness is something to be proud of.

MICHAEL PHELPS FUN FACTS

- Michael Phelps once competed against a great white shark in a 100-meter race, showing how he isn't afraid of anything.

- With an impressive wingspan of 6 feet 7 inches, Michael had a clear natural advantage over other swimmers he competed against.
- World-famous for his flawless butterfly technique, Phelps revolutionized the stroke and set a new standard for future generations of swimmers.
- Michael went to the Olympics for the first time at just age 15!
- Michael founded the Michael Phelps Foundation, an organization that promotes healthy lifestyle choices and water safety.
- During his prime, Michael signed major endorsement deals with brands like Nike, Speedo, and Visa.
- Michael's path to becoming the most decorated Olympian ever was captured on film in a documentary called *The Phelps Phenomenon*. It's really worth seeing.

THINGS TO THINK ABOUT

- Ever wonder what hurdles Michael Phelps had to splash through on his way to being the ultimate Olympian? How can his "never give up" attitude inspire you when you're facing your own challenges in life?
- Imagine you're diving into your biggest goal just like Michael dives into the pool. How can his dedication pump you up to chase after your dreams?
- Mental health matters, even for champions like Phelps. How can being honest about the tough times you're going through make you feel more comfortable talking about your feelings?

UP NEXT

As we close this chapter on Michael Phelps's awe-inspiring journey to swimming success, it's now time to turn to the next remarkable athlete. Get ready to swing on into the world of competitive gymnastics with Simone Biles.

Chapter 2

SIMONE BILES

> *I was built this way for a reason, so I'm going to use it.*
> —SIMONE BILES

Simone's story is not just about medals and records; it's about resilience, determination, and embracing who you are. Simone faced many challenges in life from a young age. Yet, she turned every obstacle into an opportunity, showcasing her strength both on and off the gymnastics floor. Let's learn Simone's story and discover what makes her such an inspirational figure for young athletes around the world.

SIMONE'S STORY

Simone Biles was born in Columbus, Ohio, and her early life was marked by challenges. Simone, along with her siblings were placed in foster care due to their mother's struggles with substance abuse disorder. Fortunately, Simone and her little sister Adria got taken in by their grandparents, Ronald and Nellie, who provided a stable and loving home.

At six years old, during a school field trip, Simone first discovered gymnastics. She was instantly hooked on the flashy sport! Simone started taking classes at Bannon's Gymnastix, and her natural talent and fearless attitude quickly caught the attention of the coaches. From that point on, her path to greatness began to unfold.

Despite the adversities she faced in her early years, Simone found strength and unwavering support within her family. Her grandparents encouraged her passion for gymnastics, creating an environment where she was free to develop personally and athletically.

Simone's journey in gymnastics was not without its obstacles. She faced various injuries and setbacks during competitions. However, her determination and perseverance helped her overcome these challenges, propelling her to the top of her sport.

Simone's accomplishments as an Olympian are nothing short of legendary. At the 2016 Rio Olympics, she won four gold medals in the individual all-around, vault, floor exercise, and team events. She also managed to get a bronze medal on the balance beam, showing her exceptional talent and hard work to the entire world. Her performance at the Rio Olympics boosted her standing as an international athlete and allowed her to be recognized as one of the greatest gymnasts in history.

After her amazing performance at the 2016 Rio Olympics, Simone took a break from gymnastics. During this time, she revealed that she had been a victim of Larry Nassar, the former USA Gymnastics team doctor. Her courage in speaking out inspired many others, bringing more attention to abuse in sports and showing young sports fans all across the world that it's never right when grown-ups touch us in bad places. If it ever happens, you have to tell someone at school, your parents, or the police right away.

Despite the challenges she faced after being touched inappropriately by someone she had once trusted, Simone returned to gymnastics with an indomitable spirit. In 2018, she made a historic comeback, winning all five events at the U.S. National Championships, a feat that hadn't been accomplished in nearly 25 years. Her ability to overcome personal and professional obstacles has made her a symbol of strength for many young women in sports.

In 2021, during the Tokyo Olympics, Simone faced another really big challenge. She got a bad case of something called "the twisties," a mental block that affects a gymnast's spatial awareness, making it difficult to spin around and nail landings like they usually do.

After facing continued struggles with the twisties, Simone made the difficult decision to withdraw from several events to prioritize her mental health. Her openness about her struggles brought global attention to the importance of mental health, especially for athletes.

Beyond the Olympics, Simone has dominated the World Championships, amassing a record number of medals and breaking numerous records. Her creative routines, including the signature "Biles" moves on the floor exercise and vault, have redefined gymnastics, setting new standards for future generations of gymnasts.

Simone Biles has become a trailblazer for diversity and representation as an African American in a predominantly white sport. Her success and visibility have inspired young athletes from all backgrounds to pursue their dreams, breaking stereotypes and challenging norms.

Simone's influence extends beyond the world of gymnastics. She has become an advocate for mental health awareness and support. Through her foundation, she works to promote a healthy lifestyle and provide opportunities for young people to engage in sports. Her dedication to giving back to the community and supporting others underscores her legacy not just as an athlete but also as a compassionate and inspiring leader.

Simone's path to Olympic success reminds us that true strength comes from overcoming adversity, embracing our uniqueness, and using our experiences to help and inspire others. Her determination, creativity, and amazing skills across gymnastic disciplines have earned her countless medals and helped her carve out a lasting legacy in the world of gymnastics.

Simone's career as a competitive gymnast continues to inspire and empower others, proving that with hard work and a little grit, anything is possible. Her story shows us the true meaning of resilience. From her early childhood challenges to facing injuries and setbacks in her gymnastics career, Simone has always bounced back stronger than ever. She shows us that no matter what obstacles come our way, we can overcome them with determination and hard work. Just like Simone, we can rise above difficulties and reach for our dreams, proving that nothing can hold us back.

Simone's story teaches us to challenge expectations and show the world what we're truly capable of. Despite being in a sport where few expected her to succeed due to her background, Simone shattered stereotypes and became one of the greatest gymnasts of all time. Her story inspires us to break free from what others might think and pursue our passions with confidence. No matter where we come from or what others say, we can achieve greatness by believing in ourselves and our abilities.

Finally, her path to Olympic glory shows us the importance of leaning on support from those who care about us. Throughout her journey, Simone relied on her grandparents, siblings, and coaches for encouragement and guidance. She reminds us that it's okay to ask for help and that we should always make an effort to surround ourselves with people who believe in us. By having a strong support system, we can face challenges more confidently and achieve our goals, just like Simone did.

SIMONE BILES FUN FACTS

- Simone has won the most medals of any American gymnast in history, having been awarded a total of 30 between both the Olympics and the World Championship of Gymnastics (*48 Facts about Simone Biles*, 2023).
- Simone won the Laureus World Sports Award for Sportswoman of the Year on four different occasions! She has also won the ESPY Award for Best Female Athlete multiple times.
- At just 4' 9", Simone was the shortest of all the athletes who competed for the U.S. in the 2016 Rio Olympics. There were 555 in total (Escobar, 2016).
- Simone loves music and often shares her favorite songs and playlists with her followers. She also has her own YouTube channel where she connects with fans by sharing training tips and glimpses into her personal life. It's worth checking out.
- Simone has been endorsed by and collaborated with different brands including Nike and Athleta.

THINGS TO THINK ABOUT

- What hurdles did Simone Biles jump over on her way to gymnastic greatness? How can her bounce-back attitude inspire you when facing tough stuff?
- Simone Biles flips the script on stereotypes in gymnastics! How does her story make you want to break the mold and be uniquely you?
- Simone's story shows us that even champions have tough days. What can you do when you get the twisties to help yourself bounce back and keep shining bright?

UP NEXT

It's time to lace up our running shoes and get ready to sprint into the next chapter. Who's joining us? None other than Usain Bolt. Step into the world of track and field, where every moment is charged with thrill and possibility!

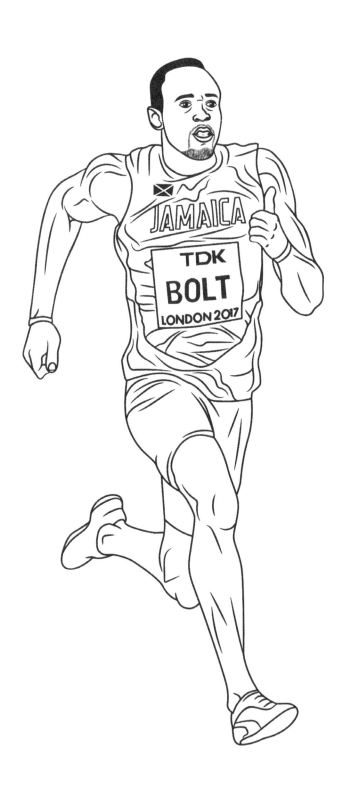

Chapter 3

USAIN BOLT

> 66 *There are better starters than me but I'm a strong finisher.*
>
> –USAIN BOLT

Imagine being known as the fastest person on Earth. That's Usain Bolt, a legend whose incredible speed made history. But what's truly inspiring about Bolt isn't just the amazing speeds he can reach, it's the way he made it to Olympic glory.

Born in a small town in Jamaica, Bolt faced many challenges and setbacks. Yet, his determination and resilience helped him overcome these obstacles and become a global icon.

Usain's story teaches us the importance of finishing strong no matter how you start. So, get ready to dive into his electrifying world of fast-paced action, where every race is a testament to hard work, humility, and the pursuit of athletic greatness.

USAIN'S STORY

Born in Jamaica, Usain Bolt ran at an amazing speed from a young age. When he was a kid, though, he was much more likely to be found playing his favorite sports, cricket and soccer, than competing in track and field events. Usain's cricket coach was the first one to see his potential as a sprinter and encourage him to try out for track and field.

The coach's suggestion set Bolt on the path to greatness. He quickly rose through the ranks, impressing coaches and scouts with his extraordinary talent. At just 15, he won the 200-meter gold at the 2002 World Junior Championships, becoming the youngest-ever male to have won any single event in the series (Lindstrom, 2019).

Despite successes early on, Bolt faced significant challenges, including hamstring injuries and scoliosis, which caused a curvature in his spine. This, combined with a difference in the length of his legs, posed some problems for the young runner. However, Bolt's determination and the support of his dedicated team of coaches and medical professionals helped him overcome these physical setbacks. His rehabilitation and relentless training were crucial in his path to recovery and eventual success.

Throughout his career, Bolt faced doubts and criticism. Early on, some questioned his dedication and work ethic, labeling him as lazy. Rather than being discouraged, Usain used these criticisms as motivation. His ability to prove his detractors wrong became a driving force in his pursuit of excellence.

The truth was, Usain wasn't lazy at all! His training regimen was as rigorous and intense as you might imagine for the fastest man alive. He would do a mix of sprint drills, strength training, and endurance workouts designed to enhance his speed, power, and agility. His workouts were carefully crafted by his coach, Glen Mills, to maximize his explosive capabilities while still maintaining his overall fitness and preventing injuries.

Usain's breakthrough came at the 2008 Beijing Olympics, where he won gold in the 100-meter, 200-meter, and 4x100-meter relay. This made him the first athlete to set world records in all three of these events (Lindstrom, 2019).

His unprecedented success continued at the 2012 London Olympics and the 2016 Rio Olympics, where he repeated his triple-gold medal performances, solidifying his status as a global icon. These victories established him as one of the greatest athletes in Olympic history!

Usain's dominance on the track is further supported by world records he set outside of the Olympics. For instance, he set the 100-meter world record at 9.58 seconds and the 200-meter record at 19.19 seconds (Lindstrom, 2019) during the 2009 World Championships in Berlin. These records remain unbroken, showing his extraordinary speed and athleticism.

Bolt's charismatic personality and genuine love for the sport endeared him to fans worldwide. His signature "Lightning Bolt" pose and infectious smile became symbols of his success and joy in athletics. His sportsmanship and humility made him a beloved figure, respected by competitors and adored by fans.

Despite his fame and success, Bolt remained humble and grounded. He consistently showed respect for his competitors and gratitude for his supporters, embodying the true spirit of sportsmanship.

Off the track, Bolt has pursued various interests and ventures. He even tried his hand at professional soccer, fulfilling a childhood dream. Although his stint was brief, it must have been really fun for him to play his favorite sport professionally. Bolt has also been active in the media, appearing in numerous television shows and documentaries that highlight his journey and personality. An animated short film about his career called *The Boy Who Learned to Fly*, offers an inspirational glimpse into his life and the challenges he overcame. It's really worth watching.

Since leaving competitive running, Bolt has turned his attention to inspiring the next generation of athletes. He established a foundation in his name that works on creating opportunities through education and cultural initiatives in his native Jamaica. Bolt's legacy goes way beyond the records he set as he continues to impact his community positively and inspire young athletes to pursue their dreams.

Usain Bolt's story is a powerful reminder that with talent, hard work, and humility, we can achieve greatness while still staying true to ourselves and uplifting others along the way. His incredible path to success as an Olympian teaches us that big dreams can take you anywhere. His story shows us that no matter where we begin, we should always dream big and believe in our potential. By setting our sights high and chasing our dreams, we can achieve extraordinary things, just like he did.

Usain's amazing speed didn't just develop overnight; it actually took a lot of hard work and dedication. Behind every lightning-fast race were countless hours of training, sweat, and effort. His story shows us that anything is possible with hard work and perseverance. If we're willing to put in the time and effort, we can reach our goals and achieve greatness in whatever we set our minds to.

Despite being the fastest man in the world, Usain Bolt remained down-to-earth and humble. He always showed respect for his competitors and gratitude for his supporters. Bolt's humility teaches us that true greatness is about more than just winning; it's about being kind, respectful, and grounded. No matter how successful we become, staying humble and appreciating others is what truly defines our character.

USAIN BOLT FUN FACTS

- Bolt loves to eat chicken nuggets and yams and jokingly credited these foods to his success at the 2008 Beijing Olympics. Though chicken nuggets aren't very healthy, yams are packed full of vital vitamins and minerals that can help you run fast just like Usain.

- Usain Bolt won the 100-meter final with a record-breaking time of 9.69 seconds during the Beijing Olympics. He did it all with his shoelace untied (Biradar, 2016)!
- Usain created a famous pose called 'To Di World' which he unleashed on the crowds of spectators at the Beijing Olympics 2008.
- Standing at 6' 5" (Shapiro, 2023), Bolt's height gives him a unique edge in sprinting, combining long strides with rapid speed.
- Usain earns around $23 million (Biradar, 2016) per year through endorsements with major brands including Puma, Virgin, and Gatorade.

THINGS TO THINK ABOUT

- Usain Bolt always gives his all, whether he's winning or facing setbacks. How can you apply his "never give up" attitude to your own challenges and goals?
- If you were to create your own signature victory pose, inspired by Usain Bolt's "Lightning Bolt," what would it look like? How does expressing confidence and joy help you feel empowered in your own achievements?
- Usain Bolt's sportsmanship and humility make him a role model both on and off the track. How can you show respect and kindness to others, even when competing or facing tough situations?

UP NEXT

As we turn the page on the extraordinary achievements of Usain Bolt, it's clear that his blend of natural talent, relentless training, and unwavering mental strength made him a legend in the world of athletics.

Hold onto your hats because we're about to dash from the track with Usain Bolt straight to the snow-covered slopes with one of the greatest snowboarders ever: Shaun White!

Chapter 4

SHAUN WHITE

66 *I didn't set out to beat the world; I just set out to do
my absolute best.*

−SHAUN WHITE

Known as "The Flying Tomato" for his vibrant red hair, Shaun has become an icon in winter sports for his impressive athletic feats and his friendly competitive spirit. His story is one about overcoming obstacles, pushing boundaries, and continually striving to be the best version of himself. So, strap on those bindings, and let's jump on the lift as we start learning about the achievements of this extraordinary athlete.

SHAUN'S STORY

Shaun White was born in San Diego, California, but there was something wrong with baby Shaun. He was born with a defective heart, and he had to get two surgeries when he was just an infant!

Despite the challenges he faced early on in life, he got stronger and grew up like any normal kid. This early battle with congenital problems didn't stop Shaun; instead, it seemed to fuel his adventurous spirit. Shaun showed an early affinity for action sports and was influenced by his older brother, Jesse, who introduced him to skateboarding.

Shaun first discovered snowboarding at age 6 during family trips to Lake Tahoe, where he quickly showed exceptional talent with the sport. He would carve down mountains like it was nothing for the little tyke, leaving an impression on anyone who saw him.

When Shaun discovered freestyle snowboarding and first tried out the half-pipe, he was even more hooked on the sport. His natural talent and fearlessness in pulling off insane tricks were clear early on. By age 7, he had already won his first snowboarding competition and began turning heads in the amateur circuit.

Shaun's dedication and skill led to five national titles before he turned professional at the tender age of 13. His debut at the Winter X Games in 2000 marked the beginning of a career filled with remarkable achievements.

Shaun went to Carlsbad High School while balancing his burgeoning snowboarding career. Southern California with its hot temperatures year-round was not the ideal place for the young snowboarder to practice his skills, but at least he could still skateboard all the time!

His family members were supportive and would take Shaun to Tahoe often. His family's encouragement and his own determination helped Shaun navigate the pressures of early success, ultimately leading to his rise as one of the most iconic athletes in action sports.

However, Shaun's path to greatness wasn't without obstacles. He had to deal with a lot of injuries, including broken bones and concussions. These setbacks tested his resolve, but he always bounced back stronger, pushing the limits of what was possible in snowboarding. The pressure from fans, sponsors, and the media was brutal, but Shaun thrived under it, using it to fuel his drive and creativity in the sport.

As an Olympian, Shaun White's achievements are unparalleled. He won his first Olympic gold in the halfpipe at the 2006 Winter Olympics in Turin, Italy, showing off his incredible skills and earning global recognition. He defended his title at the 2010 Vancouver Olympics with a flawless performance that included his signature move, the Double McTwist 1260.

After a disappointing fourth-place finish in Sochi in 2014, Shaun made a stunning comeback in the 2018 PyeongChang Olympics, winning his third gold medal in the halfpipe.

Shaun's dominance on the slopes wasn't just limited to the Olympics. He has a storied history in the X Games, where he's won numerous gold medals in both the halfpipe and slopestyle events. In 2012, he made history by becoming the first athlete to score a perfect 100 in the Winter X Games' superpipe.

Beyond snowboarding, Shaun White is also a superb skateboarder proving he has tons of skill on the half-pipe even without his feet strapped in! He has even won multiple X Games medals in half-pipe events. His influence goes even further than action sports alone. In addition to competing as an athlete, Shaun has ventured into entrepreneurship with his skate company Shaun White Supply Co. and with his clothing line WHY Space. He has also actively supported charitable organizations like St. Jude Children's Research Hospital and the Boys & Girls Clubs of America.

Shaun White's story is one of dedication, passion, and continuous innovation on the slopes. From surviving some pretty serious health challenges he faced as a baby to achieving unparalleled success in snowboarding and skateboarding, Shaun has consistently pushed the boundaries and inspired millions with his journey. His dedication to his craft, his go-get-em spirit, and his commitment to giving back make him a true icon in the world of sports and beyond.

Shaun White shows us that mistakes are a natural part of the journey. Throughout his career, Shaun faced many challenges and setbacks, including injuries and tough competitions. Instead of letting these mistakes hold him back, he embraced them and used them to improve. Shaun's story teaches us to see mistakes as opportunities to learn and grow, helping us become better and stronger in whatever we do.

Shaun's incredible journey reminds us that persistence pays off. He faced numerous obstacles on his way to becoming a snowboarding legend, but he never gave up. Shaun kept pushing forward no matter how tough things got. His determination and relentless effort led him to achieve amazing success. Shaun's story inspires us to keep going even when the path is difficult because persistence and hard work can lead to extraordinary achievements.

Just like Shaun White, we should be proud of who we are and stay true to our own path even if we're different because we're born with a weak heart or have red hair. Shaun's unique style and fearless attitude made him stand out in the world of snowboarding despite the way he was born. He showed us that embracing our individuality sets us up to pursue our passions. By being ourselves and following our dreams, we can make our mark and achieve great things. Shaun's story encourages us to celebrate our uniqueness and stay confident in who we are.

SHAUN WHITE FUN FACTS

- Shaun won his first Winter X Games gold medal in 2003.
- Shaun was in a movie called *Friends with Benefits* in 2011. He has also appeared on *Saturday Night Live*.
- He holds the record for the highest score in the men's halfpipe event at the Winter Olympics.

- Shaun has been featured on the covers of both Rolling Stone and ESPN Magazine.
- Shaun White has received multiple Excellence in Sports Performance Yearly (ESPY) Awards throughout his career.

THINGS TO THINK ABOUT

- Shaun White is known for his bold and daring tricks on the slopes. What's one new skill or activity you'd like to try that pushes you out of your comfort zone, and how can Shaun White's fearless attitude inspire you to take big leaps in life?
- Shaun White is famous for his creativity on the slopes. How can you transform your hobbies and interests into something unique or creative?
- When Shaun White falls, he gets back up and keeps going. Can you think of a time you did the same? How did you bounce back?

UP NEXT

From the slopes with Shaun White, we're switching gears to the sandy shores with April Ross and Alix Klineman! Get ready to ride the waves of excitement as we dive into the exciting world of beach volleyball!

Chapter 5

APRIL ROSS & ALIX KLINEMAN

66 *To be the best, you have to demand the best from yourself. The way to do that is try to be perfect.*

—APRIL ROSS

66 *When I switched (to beach), it was so much harder than how it looked. I am happy with my progress, but if people realized how many reps I've taken in the sand... From outside, it looks like I learned quickly. But so many times, I couldn't get it right. Eventually those reps paid off.*

—ALIX KLINEMAN

April Ross and Alix Klineman's respective paths to Olympic gold are great lessons in dedication to one's sport. Both athletes have faced some serious challenges and setbacks in their careers and personal lives. In their stories, we see the power of belief in yourself, hard work, and the unwavering belief that true champions can be just regular people who happened to rise up to Olympic glory.

From humble beginnings to dominating the sandy courts of Tokyo, Ross and Klineman's partnership showcases how dedication and grit can transform dreams into reality. Let's dive into the inspiring stories of these two remarkable athletes.

APRIL'S STORY

April Ross was born in Costa Mesa, California. From an early age, she showed a natural talent for volleyball, playing competitively in high school at Newport Harbor High School. Her passion for the sport only grew, leading her to a standout collegiate career at the University of Southern California (USC).

At USC, April became a three-time All-American, helping her team win consecutive AVCA national titles in 2002 and 2003. Her achievements on the court included being named the National Freshman of the Year and the 2003 PAC-10 Player of the Year.

Despite her success, Ross faced several challenges and setbacks, including injuries and defeats. However, she viewed these obstacles as opportunities for growth, constantly striving to improve her game. Balancing her athletic ambitions with academic goals, Ross graduated from USC with a degree in international relations.

Her partnership with Alix Klineman, beginning in 2017, proved to be a game-changer. Together, they achieved numerous victories, including the gold medal at the 2020 Tokyo Olympics.

Throughout her Olympic career, Ross has won a silver medal from the 2012 London Olympics playing alongside Jennifer Kessy, a bronze from the 2016 Rio Olympics for her efforts with Kerri Walsh Jennings, and a gold from the 2020 Tokyo Olympics paired with Klineman.

In addition to her Olympic success, Ross has won multiple medals at the FIVB Beach Volleyball World Championships. Her accolades and perseverance through various challenges highlight her dedication to the sport and her ability to inspire others with her great volleyball playing and positive attitude.

Ross actively supports charities, including The Side-Out Foundation for breast cancer research and Kids Play International, showing that she cares about more than just sports.

ALIX'S STORY

Alix Klineman was born in Manhattan Beach, California into a Jewish-American family. She loved playing indoor volleyball from a young age. At Mira Costa High School, she led her team to three consecutive California State Championships, earning the Gatorade National Player of the Year award in 2006. Klineman continued her impressive career at Stanford University becoming a four-time AVCA All-American and leading the team to two NCAA final matches.

After not making the U.S. Olympic Volleyball Team for the 2016 Rio Olympics, she switched to beach volleyball. This transition required her to adapt to a different playing environment and develop new skills, such as sand movement and ball control. Despite the new challenges she faced, Klineman's determination and resilience helped her establish herself as a top player in beach volleyball.

In 2017, Klineman partnered up with April Ross, marking a turning point in her career. Together, they competed in multiple tournaments and quickly became a formidable team. Their hard work and synergy paid off at the 2020 Tokyo Olympics where they won the gold medal in beach volleyball, going undefeated in match play and losing only one set throughout the entire tournament.

Klineman's achievements extend beyond the Olympics. She has won numerous medals at the FIVB Beach Volleyball World Championships and various international competitions. Her journey from indoor to beach volleyball is a testament to her adaptability, perseverance, and exceptional talent. Through her partnership with Ross and her individual accomplishments, Klineman has gained recognition and respect in the world of beach volleyball.

Alix is engaged to former NHL player Teddy Purcell, and they have a dog named Vedder together.

Both April Ross and Alix Klineman show us that adaptability is essential in overcoming challenges. Both athletes faced new environments and obstacles in their careers, but their ability to adjust and evolve helped them succeed. Their story teaches us the importance of being flexible and open to change. By embracing new experiences and learning from them, we can grow and achieve our goals, no matter what challenges come our way.

April and Alix leaned on each other for support during tough times, and their strong bond played a crucial role in their success. Their partnership attests to the importance of surrounding ourselves with people who believe in us and lift us up. Having a supportive team or friends can make a big difference in our lives, helping us stay motivated and overcome difficulties. Just like April and Alix, we should cherish and nurture the supportive relationships in our lives.

Through all the highs and lows, April Ross and Alix Klineman found joy in their journey. They remind us that the process of working toward our goals is just as important as the outcome. By cherishing every moment and finding happiness in the pursuit of our dreams, we can lead more fulfilling and joyful lives. April and Alix's story encourages us to enjoy the ride, celebrate our progress, and make the most of every experience along the way.

APRIL ROSS AND ALIX KLINEMAN FUN FACTS

- April Ross had the great honor of being chosen as the flag bearer for the United States during the closing ceremony of the 2020 Tokyo Olympics.
- April's mother is Dutch, so she holds dual citizenship in the U.S. and the Netherlands.
- April not only excelled at athletics but also at academics. She graduated from USC with a degree in International Relations and later pursued a master's degree in business administration.

- Alix Klineman is also somewhat of a genius. Not only did she skip first grade, but she also graduated from Stanford!
- Alix and April met at the Stagecoach country music festival in 2017.
- Alix is the taller of the two at a stunning 6' 5" (Burack, 2021).

THINGS TO THINK ABOUT

- April Ross and Alix Klineman rocked the beach volleyball court as a team. Think about a time you rocked teamwork with your friends. What made it awesome, and how can you bring that energy to other activities?
- April Ross and Alix Klineman faced challenges but kept smashing goals. Can you think of a time when you faced a tough moment but kept going? How did you bounce back, and what did you learn from it?
- April Ross and Alix Klineman dreamed big and made waves in beach volleyball. What's a big dream you have? How can their story inspire you to chase it with all your heart?

UP NEXT

From the sun-kissed sands with April Ross and Alix Klineman, let's sprint into the history books with the legendary Jesse Owens! Get ready to explore the remarkable achievements of the man who is perhaps the greatest track and field athlete of all time, one who made history by breaking Olympic barriers and asserting the power of racial equality against the rising tide of fascism in Europe.

Chapter 6

JESSE OWENS

> 66 *The battles that count aren't the ones for gold medals. The struggles within yourself - the invisible, inevitable battles inside all of us - that's where it's at.*
>
> –JESSE OWENS

Jesse Owens's legacy in sports and as a symbol of racial harmony worldwide goes way beyond his athletic achievements. Born in an era of intense racial discrimination, Owens faced many steep challenges in life, ones that tested his spirit and determination. Yet, his inner battles and unwavering resolve propelled him to defy the odds stacked against him and etch his name in history as a symbol of excellence and courage in the face of brutal persecution.

This chapter is all about the extraordinary life of Jesse Owens, tracing his path along the track, from humble beginnings to global renown. It's also a story about the lessons we can learn from history and the importance of facing both our internal and external struggles with grace and determination.

JESSE'S STORY

Jesse Owens was born in Oakville, Alabama. He was the youngest of ten children in a sharecropping family that worked hard in the fields.

His family used to call him "J.C.," short for James Cleveland—his first and middle names on his birth certificate.

Though slavery had long been abolished, agricultural workers in the South still lived under very poor conditions and were stuck in grinding poverty. At nine, his family decided to leave the harsh realities of the South and moved up North to Cleveland, Ohio. Jesse settled into his new school there and found it to be mighty fine.

When this young boy showed up to class, his teacher pronounced "J.C." as "Jesse," so the name stuck, and everyone just called him Jesse from that point on. Owens discovered his talent for running at a young age and quickly gained recognition for his speed and agility. In high school, Jesse was a standout athlete, winning three events at the 1933 National Interscholastic Championships.

Jesse went off to Ohio State University, where he set multiple records in track and field events despite facing racial discrimination and financial hardships. Known as the "Buckeye Bullet," Owens, along with his other African American classmates were banned from on-campus housing and faced segregation in the dining facilities. Jesse worked various jobs to support himself while continuing to train and compete.

In the 1936 Berlin Olympics, Jesse went from being a fast kid on the track to becoming an international icon. His appearance at the games was very meaningful given the sociopolitical climate in Europe at the time.

Adolf Hitler, the leader of the Nazi party, aimed to use the Olympic Games to promote his theories of racial superiority, asserting the supposed dominance of the Aryan race over other populations all around the world. Owens, an African American athlete, directly challenged and debunked these racist ideologies by winning four gold medals.

His victories in the 100-meter, 200-meter, long jump, and 4x100-meter relay not only demonstrated his exceptional talent but also struck a powerful blow against the Nazi propaganda, symbolizing the triumph of the human spirit and equality over the bigotry and hatred that the Nazis tried to spread all over Europe.

Throughout his career, Owens set numerous world records, including the ones for the 220-yard dash, 220-yard low hurdles, and long jump. His achievements in a single day at the 1935 Big Ten meet where he broke a total of five world records and tied another one, all in just 45 minutes, is still considered one of the greatest one-day performances in sports history (Gay, 2023).

Owens continued to face financial difficulties as well as racial discrimination even after his success at the Olympics. He took on various jobs, including publicity stunts such as racing against horses to get extra money to help support his family. Despite things not working out in life for Jessee, he continued to contribute to society through public relations work, goodwill tours, and advocacy for youth and sports.

Jesse Owens's story is one of defiance and the power of self-belief. His legacy continues to inspire generations, reminding us that even those who make history aren't always treated with respect and dignity or given opportunities. Jesse was ahead of his time, and it would take decades before the Olympics became a venue that largely celebrates international and racial diversity.

One other important takeaway from Jesse Owens's story is that challenges need to be confronted directly. Even in the face of intense racial discrimination, Jesse never backed down. He stood tall and competed with determination, breaking barriers and setting new standards in athletics. His story shows us that facing challenges head-on can help us overcome obstacles and make a significant impact no matter the difficulties we encounter.

Jesse Owens' path to becoming a legend was built on hard work and dedication. He didn't achieve greatness overnight; it took years of relentless training and effort. His story reminds us that hard work pays off in the end. By putting in the time and effort and staying committed to our goals, we can achieve remarkable success in whatever we pursue.

Owens' confidence and self-belief drove him to achieve extraordinary feats, including winning four gold medals at the 1936 Berlin Olympics. His story inspires us to trust in our abilities and never give up on our dreams. When we have an unwavering belief in ourselves, we can overcome any challenge and reach our fullest potential.

JESSE OWENS FUN FACTS

- Even though U.S. President Franklin D. Roosevelt was known for his progressive policies, he refused to invite Jesse Owens to the White House, showing how racism was still very present at the highest levels of power in the U.S. at that time.
- One time, Jesse's mother had to perform makeshift surgery on him with a knife! OWWWWWIEEEEEE! It just shows you how poor they were that they couldn't even afford to visit a doctor.
- Owens wasn't much of a baseball player himself, but that didn't stop him from being hired as a running coach for the New York Mets to improve players' base-running techniques.

THINGS TO THINK ABOUT

- When have you felt the heat to shine? How did you handle it, and what can you learn from Jesse Owens's cool moves under pressure?

- How can sports be a game-changer for fairness and fun? What's Jesse Owens's secret play for justice?
- How can Jesse Owens's superhero-style bravery inspire you to shake things up?

UP NEXT

We've sprinted alongside Jesse Owens, and it's now time to trade in our running shoes for a pair of ice skates and glide along with the incredible Nathan Chen!

Nathan, known for his technical figure skating skills and his high level of artistic expression, has redefined the sport with his innovative performances and relentless dedication. So, get ready to be amazed by his path from a young skating prodigy to an Olympic champion, showing off the perfect blend of athleticism and grace on ice to adoring fans all over the world!

Chapter 7

NATHAN CHEN

> ❝ *You have to have passion for what you do, or else it's difficult when the going gets tough.*
>
> —NATHAN CHEN

Nathan Chen cut graceful lines across the ice until he made his dream of becoming an Olympic gold medalist come true. His dedication, natural talent, and charismatic presence in the competitive rink have set him apart as one of the top athletes in the sport. This chapter is all about Nathan's inspiring story, highlighting his early beginnings and triumphs and the lessons learned from his incredible journey on the ice.

NATHAN'S STORY

Nathan Chen was born in Salt Lake City, Utah, to a Chinese American family. He was the youngest of five siblings. At age 3, inspired by his older brothers playing ice hockey, he first stepped onto the ice, initially aspiring to be a hockey goalie. He soon switched gears and set eyes on his passion: figure skating!

Nathan joined the Salt Lake Figure Skating, a club where his natural talent and dedication quickly set him apart. By 2010 and 2011, Chen had already claimed national titles at the novice level and became the national junior champion in 2012.

Nathan's journey wasn't without its challenges. He injured his hip in 2015, which forced him out of professional competition for much of the following year. The year ended up offering some much-needed time off for Nathan, and he used it to focus on off-ice training at U.S. Olympic facilities.

This period of recovery and strengthening proved to be really useful as Chen returned to the ice stronger than ever! At the 2017 U.S. Figure Skating Championships, he made history by becoming the first male skater to land five quadruple jumps in a single performance. Nathan won the competition, and it was the first of what would be a total of six consecutive national titles that stretched from 2017 to 2022.

Nathan Chen's dedication to figure skating didn't hinder his academic pursuits. In 2018, he enrolled at Yale University, majoring in statistics and data science. Balancing a rigorous academic schedule with his demanding training regimen, he demonstrated unbelievable time management skills and discipline.

His time at the Ivy League university also influenced his skating, as he incorporated elements from his coursework into his routines. For instance, a music class he took inspired his use of a piece composed by minimalist composer Philip Glass for his free skate at the 2021 World Championships. Despite taking a leave of absence to focus on the 2022 Beijing Olympics, Nathan's commitment to education remains a significant aspect of his life, highlighting the importance of balancing multiple passions.

Nathan's Olympic career began at the 2018 Winter Games in Pyeongchang, South Korea. Despite a disappointing 17th place after the short program, he made a remarkable comeback in the free skate, landing an Olympic-record six quadruple jumps, which won him the free skate portion and placed him fifth overall in the singles competition. He contributed to the U.S. team's bronze medal in the mixed-team event.

Nathan's determination to continue pursuing Olympic greatness was strong. He trained hard, knowing that it would pay off big-time one day. He was right! He won his first world title in 2018 and defended it in 2019 and 2021, becoming the first male figure skater from the U.S. to win three world titles in a row since Scott Hamilton.

In preparation for the 2022 Winter Olympics in Beijing, Nathan took a leave of absence from Yale University. His hard work paid off as he set a world record in the short program and won the gold medal in the free skate, securing his place as the Olympic champion with a combined score of 332.60 (*Nathan Chen*, n.d.).

Nathan Chen's journey to the top of his sport gives us a clear example of how his passion, talent, and perseverance contributed to his resounding success. His ability to overcome setbacks and maintain a balance between his academic pursuits and skating career makes his story truly inspiring.

Though Nathan wears fancy costumes made by the womenswear designer Vera Wang, studied ballet, and has long participated in a sport he controversially called "homosexual-dominated," he has made it clear publicly that he is not gay. Nathan actually caught some flak for his characterization of his own sport as being "gay", but he later apologized for it. Like his favorite musical artist Eminem, he shows us that sometimes people's words are misconstrued by the public.

This just goes to show that even in sports like figure skating and venues like the Olympics, there's still a lot of work to do when it comes to gender equality and LGBTQ+ rights. It also shows us that anyone can be a figure skater no matter who they are or where they come from.

Nathan Chen's path to skating success teaches us the importance of persistence. He faced challenges and setbacks, including injuries, but he never gave up on his goals. Nathan's story shows that sticking with your dreams, even when things get tough, can result in incredible achievements. His determination to keep trying, no matter the obstacles, reminds us that perseverance is key to success.

Nathan's unique style on the ice was another factor that helped him succeed. It teaches us to think outside the box and try new things. His innovative routines and artistic expression set him apart in the world of figure skating. Nathan's story encourages us to embrace our creativity and be bold in our pursuits. By thinking creatively and trying new approaches, we can achieve remarkable results and stand out in our own ways.

Nathan Chen is a great example of balancing passions and responsibilities. While excelling in figure skating, he also pursued his education. Nathan's ability to juggle his rigorous training schedule with academic commitments shows us the importance of finding balance in our own lives. His story inspires us to manage our time effectively and prioritize our goals, ensuring we can succeed in a wide range of pursuits.

NATHAN CHEN FUN FACTS

- Nathan trained at the Ballet West Academy for nearly seven years, enhancing his grace and artistry on the ice.
- Nathan credits much of his success to his mother who supported his skating journey from the beginning.

- Asian American figure skaters Michelle Kwan and Kristi Yamaguchi inspired Chen to pursue his dreams (Weaver, 2018).
- Nathan is the first male figure skater to land five quadruple jumps in a single program (*Nathan Chen*, 2022).
- Nathan says he views figure skating as a "passion project" rather than just a sports career (Weaver, 2018).
- Before every competition, Nathan always puts on his left skate before his right due to superstition.

THINGS TO THINK ABOUT

- Ever tripped and turned it into a trick? What can you learn from Nathan Chen's epic fails-turned-flips?
- How do you juggle your passions? What ninja moves can you learn from Nathan Chen to master your time?
- Who's your cheer squad? How can Nathan Chen's dream team help you reach new heights?

UP NEXT

Now that we've twirled on the ice with Nathan Chen, let's dive into the pool with the unstoppable Katie Ledecky! Known for her incredible endurance and unmatched swimming skills, Katie has set records and dominated competitions around the world.

Get ready to be inspired by her journey, her dedication to the sport, and her pursuit of Olympic glory. As we explore her story, we'll see how she has become one of the greatest swimmers of all time.

Chapter 8

KATIE LEDECKY

> 66 *I would encourage you to set really high goals. Set goals that, when you set them, you think they're impossible. But then every day you can work towards them, and anything is possible, so keep working hard and follow your dreams.*
>
> –KATIE LEDECKY

Katie Ledecky isn't just any old swimmer—she's a symbol of Olympic excellence. Katie's journey in swimming began at a young age. Her incredible determination and relentless work ethic propelled her to become one of the greatest swimmers in history.

From breaking records to winning multiple Olympic gold medals, Katie's story is about the power of hard work and big dreams. Her path to glory inspires us to push beyond our limits and strive for greatness in everything we do. Let's learn the story of a true champion, a true champion in the pool and beyond.

KATIE'S STORY

Katie Ledecky was born in Washington, D.C. She started swimming at age 6, inspired by her mother who was a competitive swimmer herself when she was in college.

Growing up in Bethesda, Maryland, Katie found a passion for swimming early on, often training with her older brother, Michael. Her early love for the water quickly formed a competitive edge as she joined local swim clubs and began to dominate age-group competitions. Katie's parents valued both education and athletics. They encouraged a balanced approach to life, emphasizing the importance of academic excellence alongside sports.

Her high school years were filled with early morning practices, schoolwork, and evening training sessions, a routine that required immense discipline and dedication. This rigorous schedule prepared her well for her future endeavors.

Despite her rigorous training schedule, Katie managed to balance her academic pursuits with her swimming career. She attended a private Catholic school in Maryland, where she excelled academically while maintaining her intense Olympian training regimen.

Katie's breakthrough came at the 2012 London Olympics when, at just 15 years old, she won the gold medal in the 800-meter freestyle. This victory made her one of the youngest American swimmers to win an Olympic gold medal. Her performance was a sign of things to come as she continued to break records and win titles.

In 2013, Katie set world records in the 800-meter and 1500-meter freestyle at the World Championships, solidifying her status as a dominant force in swimming.

After all that success, she earned an athletic scholarship to Stanford University, where she continued to break collegiate records while pursuing a degree in psychology with a minor in political science. Her time management and dedication allowed her to thrive both in the classroom and the pool. Known for her incredible work ethic, Katie's training includes intense pool workouts, strength training, and conditioning exercises, allowing her to maintain top performance.

During college, Katie continued to shine, winning eight National Collegiate Athletic Association (NCAA) titles and setting an impressive 15 NCAA records. She was instrumental in leading her team to back-to-back NCAA Team Championships and two consecutive Pac-12 Conference Team Championships.

Throughout her career, Katie faced immense pressure to perform at every competition. Her ability to remain composed and focused under such pressure shows just how much mental strength she has. Whether setting new world records or competing in high-stakes races, Katie's composure under the intense spotlight of high-stakes competition and her consistent performance in events show us her deep levels of mastery of the sport and her pure determination to keep competing.

Katie Ledecky's Olympic career has been nothing short of legendary. At the 2016 Rio Games, she won gold medals in the 200 and 800-meter freestyle events and the 4x200-meter freestyle relay, along with a silver medal in the 4x100-meter freestyle relay. This made a total of three golds and one silver. She also managed to set world records in both the 400-meter and 800-meter freestyle events during these games.

At the 2020 Tokyo Olympics, she added to her medal tally with golds in the 800-meter and 1500-meter freestyle and silvers in the 400-meter freestyle and the 4x200-meter freestyle relay. Her dominance in long-distance events is particularly notable with an unbeaten streak in the 800-meter freestyle for over a decade.

Katie's path to swimming success has been marked by her unparalleled achievements and the challenges she overcame to reach the pinnacle of her sport. Her story shows us how with a bit of passion, hard work, and determination, we too can achieve extraordinary success.

She credits much of her success to her supportive family, especially her mother, who was her first coach and remains a big influence in her life. The encouragement and guidance from her family provided a strong foundation, allowing Katie to pursue her dreams with confidence. Her journey shows us how having a really strong support system helps us a lot when we're trying to achieve big goals.

Katie speaks openly about the importance of mental health in athletics, advocating for resources and support for athletes' well-being. She has also used her platform to support various charitable causes, emphasizing the importance of giving back to the community.

Her humility teaches us to appreciate success while treating others with kindness and respect. Despite her numerous accomplishments and world records, Katie remains down-to-earth and grateful. Her story shows us that no matter how successful we become, it's important to stay humble and kind to those around us. Katie's grounded nature reminds us that true greatness is reflected in how we treat others.

Whether it's breaking world records or balancing her athletic career with academic pursuits, Katie faces every challenge with courage and determination. Her bravery inspires us to tackle new challenges head-on and grow from them, and her story encourages us to embrace difficult situations as opportunities to learn and improve. By confronting challenges with a positive attitude, we can grow stronger and achieve our goals.

Katie's incredible path to Olympic success reminds us to aim high and believe in ourselves. She set big goals and worked tirelessly to achieve them, showing us that anything is possible with hard work and dedication. Katie's journey inspires us to dream big and pursue our passions with all our might. By believing in ourselves and giving our best effort, we can turn our dreams into reality and reach new heights.

KATIE LEDECKY FUN FACTS

- At just 15, Katie was the youngest member of the U.S. Olympic swimming team at the 2012 London Games. She won her first gold medal there in the 800-meter freestyle.
- In addition to the 400-meter and 800-meter records she set at the 2016 Rio Games, Katie holds the record for the 1500-meter freestyle event. Her dominance in both short and long-distance races is unparalleled.
- Katie Ledecky is known for her versatility in different distances, excelling both in sprint and freestyle events.

THINGS TO THINK ABOUT

- Ever felt the heat? How can you keep your cool like Katie Ledecky when the pressure is on?
- How do you juggle your time? What splashtastic time management tips can you borrow from Katie Ledecky?
- What's your big goal? How can Katie Ledecky's "dive in and go for it" attitude inspire you to chase it?

UP NEXT

From making waves with Katie Ledecky in the pool; now, let's leap onto the gymnastics mat with the legendary Nadia Comaneci!

Just as Katie's dedication and hard work have redefined swimming today, Nadia's incredible journey revolutionized gymnastics in her time. Her perfect scores and groundbreaking performances set a new standard in the sport, inspiring generations of gymnasts up to the present day. As we transition from the water to the mat, prepare to meet a true Olympic icon in every sense.

Chapter 9

NADIA COMANECI

 I don't run away from a challenge because I am afraid. Instead, I run toward it because the only way to escape fear is to trample it beneath your feet.

–NADIA COMANECI

Nadia Comaneci's path to international sports stardom, starting out as a gymnast from a small town in Romania to becoming one of the greatest gymnasts of all time, is a story of unparalleled dedication and courage. Nadia started to excel at her sport at a very tender age and was fueled by an unwavering determination to overcome every obstacle in her path. Nadia's commitment to her craft earned her a place in the annals of Olympic history and inspired countless athletes around the world.

This chapter is all about Nadia's story. In it, we'll take a look at how her grit and perseverance led her to achieve the impossible—scoring perfect 10s and setting new standards in gymnastics. Through her story, we'll learn the power of hard work, the importance of facing challenges head-on, and the big impact that just one person can have on an entire sport.

NADIA'S STORY

Nadia Comaneci was born in Gheorghe Gheorghiu-Dej, Romania. Her obsession with gymnastics started early. She was a bit hyperactive and had a fascination with movement from a very young age. She had a boundless energy that needed an outlet, and her parents were eager to help her channel all that energy positively. At age 6, her talent was discovered by Béla Károlyi, the gymnastics coach who would later come to be an important presence in her life and career.

Nadia trained under the watchful eyes of Béla and his wife, who were both instrumental in shaping her into a world-class gymnast. She spent countless hours perfecting her routines, enduring rigorous training sessions that demanded both physical endurance and mental resilience. Nadia's childhood was far from typical; while other children played, she was in the gym, honing her skills and dreaming of Olympic glory.

Nadia quickly rose to prominence in the gymnastics world. By the time she was 11, she made her international debut and began turning heads with her innovative routines and flawless execution. Her performances were characterized by a blend of artistic grace and technical precision, setting her apart from her peers.

Her training regimen was intense and demanding. Under the rigorous guidance of Béla and Marta Károlyi, Nadia endured grueling training sessions that honed her skills and built her physical and mental toughness. This relentless dedication to her craft prepared her for the high-stakes world of competitive gymnastics.

The pressure to perform flawlessly was immense. Every competition brought with it the expectation of perfection, and Nadia faced this pressure head-on. Her ability to remain composed under such scrutiny helped her further solidify her mental fortitude and maintain an unwavering focus.

Nadia's accomplishments as an Olympian are nothing short of legendary. During the 1976 Montreal Olympics, at age 14, she made history by becoming the first gymnast to score a perfect 10 in an Olympic event. This unprecedented achievement wasn't a one-time occurrence; she went on to score six more perfect 10s during the same Games (*Nadia Comaneci Biography, Olympic Medals, Records and Age*, n.d.)!

Nadia won three gold medals, clinching the win for the balance beam event, the uneven bars, and the all-around competition. During the same games, she also got a silver medal in the team event and a bronze in the floor exercises. Her performances captivated the world and earned her international acclaim.

Beyond the Olympics, Nadia continued to excel at the World Championships of Gymnastics. She won tons of medals, making it clear to all that she was truly one of the greatest gymnasts of all time. Her innovative skills, such as the aerial walkover and the double twist dismount on the balance beam, left a lasting impact on the sport and continue to inspire gymnasts today.

Nadia's journey wasn't without its challenges. She faced setbacks, including a disappointing finish at the 1978 World Championships and an injury in 1979. However, she bounced back to win two more gold medals at the 1980 Moscow Olympics. Her amazing skills coupled with her determination to overcome obstacles are the key elements that came to define her remarkable career.

At the peak of Nadia's career, Romania was under the oppressive regime of Nicolae Ceaușescu. Romanian athletes, Nadia included, were often used as propaganda tools to assert the superiority of the state.

Despite her global fame, Nadia was subject to stringent controls and pressures imposed by her country's government. She faced a lot of scrutiny and was expected to perform flawlessly to uphold the image of Romania. She was monitored very closely—her training regimen being closely watched by government officials.

In addition to the pressure to excel, Nadia dealt with personal restrictions. Her movements were heavily monitored, and she had limited contact with the outside world. This isolation was part of the broader strategy to keep high-profile athletes under control and prevent them from fleeing to other countries.

In 1981, after a disappointing performance at the World Championships, rumors began to spread about the harsh conditions and emotional strain she was under in her home country. In 1989, as the Iron Curtain came down, Nadia was able to make a daring escape to the United States, seeking freedom from the oppressive regime.

Nadia Comaneci's story is one of extraordinary talent, relentless dedication, and groundbreaking achievements. Her legacy as the first gymnast to score a perfect 10 and her contributions to the sport continue to inspire athletes around the world even today.

Her path to Olympic glory teaches us the importance of stepping out of our comfort zones and embracing challenges. She wasn't afraid to tackle tough routines and push the boundaries of what was possible in gymnastics. Her courage to take on difficult tasks and perform them flawlessly reminds us that embracing challenges can lead to extraordinary achievements. By stepping up to face challenges head-on, we can grow and reach new heights in our own lives.

NADIA COMANECI FUN FACTS

- After her historic performance in 1976, Nadia continued to dominate the gymnastics scene, winning a total of nine Olympic medals throughout her career.

- Despite facing numerous challenges, including the political pressures of her home country, Nadia remained steadfast in her aspirations.
- Nadia continues to be involved in the gymnastics community as a judge, commentator, and ambassador for the sport, inspiring young gymnasts around the world.

THINGS TO THINK ABOUT

- Ever aimed for a perfect score? What was it like, and what did you learn from trying to hit the bullseye?
- Think you've smashed the system? How can Nadia's flips and twists inspire you to break the mold and seek freedom outside the forces that oppress you?
- Who's your hero and why? How can Nadia's gravity-defying feats fire up your dreams?

UP NEXT

Let's turn from the graceful flips and awe-inspiring perfection of Nadia Comaneci to the rapid-fire world of track and field where speed, strength, and agility take center stage.

Enter Carl Lewis, a legendary sprinter and long jumper whose record-breaking feats have left an indelible mark on athletics. Join us as we delve into the stories of extraordinary athletes who have pushed the boundaries of human performance, showcasing the relentless pursuit of excellence on the world's greatest stages.

Chapter 10

CARL LEWIS

> 66 *When I run—you can see my record—I run to win.*
>
> —CARL LEWIS

Carl Lewis is widely recognized as one of the greatest track and field athletes of all time. Born in Birmingham, Alabama, Carl's natural talent and passion for athletics were clear from an early age. Throughout his career, he excelled in multiple events, including sprinting, long jump, and relay races.

Carl's dedication to his craft, grueling training regimen, and positive, forward-looking attitude propelled him to become one of the most celebrated Olympians of all time, earning nine gold medals and one silver medal across four Olympic Games. This chapter is all about the sports career of Carl Lewis, from his early days and legendary Olympic achievements to his lasting legacy in the world of sports.

CARL'S STORY

Carl Lewis was born in Birmingham, Alabama. His path to athletic merit started early in life, as he had a supportive environment that encouraged his athletic talents. Carl's parents were both track and field coaches, and their background in these sports fueled Carl's early interest in athletics. This foundational support was crucial in developing his natural talent.

From a young age, Carl displayed exceptional talent in track and field. He started training seriously, focusing on sprinting and long jump, two events that would eventually define his career. In high school, Carl had already set a national high school long jump record and was on his way to greatness.

Carl's next stop was the University of Houston, where he claimed multiple NCAA titles and set numerous records, firming up his status as an exceptional athlete on the collegiate circuit. Lewis wasn't just great at track and field though—he also dabbled in other sports such as basketball and football, showing off his remarkable athletic versatility.

Furthermore, his versatility in track and field events set him apart from other athletes. From the 100-meter and 200-meter dash to the long jump, he could seemingly do it all! This unique ability to dominate in different events led some to call him the "Olympian of the Century" and "Sportsman of the Century." Carl's skills on the track were on full display in the individual events he competed in, but he also shined in relay races where he gave stellar performances.

For Carl, maintaining peak performance required grueling training sessions and strict discipline. His training regimen was very intense, and he focused hard on maximizing his speed, agility, and jumping ability. Carl's dedication to improving his craft and maximizing his performance was unwavering, contributing to his longevity and success in the sport.

Carl Lewis's most significant achievements came at the Olympic Games, where he won nine gold medals and one silver medal. At the 1984 Olympics in Los Angeles, he matched legendary track and field star Jesse Owens's feat from 1936 by taking the gold in the 100-meter and 200-meter races, the long jump, and the 4x100-meter relay. Carl's Olympic journey continued with more gold medals in the following years' games, including Seoul 1988, Barcelona 1992, and Atlanta 1996.

Throughout his career, Lewis set numerous world records in sprinting and long jump events. His performances often left audiences in awe, particularly his world record in the 100 meters and his dominance in the long jump where he won four Olympic gold medals in a row.

Carl's impact goes far beyond his athletic achievements. His namesake foundation aims to empower others, creating opportunities through education and health initiatives. His legacy has also been shaped by the work he's done as a motivational speaker and an advocate for social causes. His influence continues to inspire new generations of athletes and those aspiring to overcome their own challenges.

His story shows us the power of versatility, dedication, and the constant desire to be better. His path to Olympic glory, from a young talent in Alabama to a global sports icon, shows us what it really means to push the boundaries and become an Olympic legend.

Furthermore, it teaches us the importance of flexibility and having varied skill sets. He excelled in multiple events, including sprints and the long jump, showing off his wide range of skills. Carl's story encourages us to explore different interests and develop various talents. By being open to trying new things and diversifying our skills, we can find our strengths and achieve success in multiple areas.

Carl's rise to international superstardom came from his hard work and discipline. His story emphasizes the importance of staying dedicated and consistent in our efforts, and his rigorous training and unwavering commitment to his goals remind us that success doesn't come overnight. By putting in the effort and maintaining our discipline, we can achieve our dreams and reach our full potential.

CARL LEWIS FUN FACTS

- Though Carl is known as a track and field star, he also showed interest in basketball and football.
- Did you know that Carl tried his hand at music too? In the late 1980s, he released a pop album, even collaborating with legendary producer Quincy Jones on one of the tracks.
- Lewis became a pop culture sensation and even ventured into acting at one time, appearing in films like *Alien Hunter* and *Material Girls*, further demonstrating his talent and wide range of skills.
- Carl put his life story to paper in a book called *Inside Track: My Professional Life in Amateur Track and Field*, offering insights into his career and life.

THINGS TO THINK ABOUT

- What achievements are you proud of, and how can you celebrate your victories like Carl Lewis?
- How do you stay disciplined in your training or practice? What can you learn from Carl Lewis's dedication to his craft?
- Beyond his athletic achievements, Carl Lewis has been an advocate for social causes. How can you use your talents to make a positive impact in your community, just like Carl Lewis?

UP NEXT

Carl Lewis's journey from a young athlete in Alabama to a globally renowned sports icon is a tale of exceptional talent, versatility, and dedication. His accomplishments in track and field, spanning sprints and long jumps, have set enduring records and inspired generations of runners.

It's now time to gracefully glide to the Winter Olympics. So, strap on those skates and get out on the ice because we're going to explore the story of another extraordinary athlete. That's right! Up next, we're turning our attention to the world of figure skating, where Katarina Witt dazzled audiences with her elegance, skill, and captivating Olympic performances.

YOU

"Twenty years from now, you will be more disappointed by the things that you didn't do than by the ones you did do. So... Explore. Dream. Discover."

— MARK TWAIN

Let's pause for a moment now. Each of these chapters has been headed with a name that will be remembered for many years after the person who owns it has departed the earth. Each of them is a hero, overcoming an array of challenges and pushing themselves hard to reach their goals. You can be among them.

This doesn't mean you're necessarily going to become an Olympic athlete (or even that you want to). It doesn't mean that your name is certain to become a household name (but who's to say it won't?). No matter what your story is, you will live on long after you're gone, and you will be remembered for the things you did. Let them be the things you wanted to do. Dream big. Dream big, and do what it takes to get there, no matter how many challenges you come up against along the way.

Each of these stories is an inspiration, no matter whether you have any interest in being a gymnast, a swimmer, or a long-distance runner. Each has something to teach you about resilience, perseverance, and commitment – and that can be applied to any area of life, no matter where your dreams take you. Each of the people in this book has done far more than excel in their given sport: They've inspired us to give our best to everything we do.

This is your chance to be an inspiration too. Simply by sharing these stories, you can inspire other young people to take their dreams and run with them – to see how far they can get simply by never giving up.

By leaving a review of this book on Amazon, you'll point new readers in the direction of these incredible stories – and there's no telling what that little nugget of inspiration could do for them.

Part of an athlete's job is to be a role model, and they do it simply by sharing their stories: Each one tells us something about our own potential. By spreading the word about these stories, you'll carry on the work of these great athletes and help other people realize just how powerful they truly are.

Thank you so much for your support. Let's see who's up next, shall we?

Scan the QR code below

Chapter 11

KATARINA WITT

> 66 *Too many times women try to be competitive with each other. We should help support each other, rather than try to be better than each other.*
>
> —KATARINA WITT

Katarina Witt's journey from a young skater in East Germany to a global icon in figure skating is a testament to her dedication, talent, and power of self-expression. Known for her artistic flair and elegance on the ice, Witt not only won gold medals but also the hearts of audiences worldwide. Her path, gracefully cut out across the ice, from a young skater in East Germany to a global sports icon shows her dedication, talent, and ability to connect deeply with spectators from all across the globe. Katarina's story shows us how her unique approach to the sport set her apart and made a big impact on the world of figure skating.

KATARINA'S STORY

Katarina Witt was born in Karl-Marx-Stadt, East Germany (current-day Chemnitz, Germany). From a young age, it was clear she had a natural talent for figure skating. At just five years old, she started skating and quickly caught the attention of East German sports officials. Recognizing her potential, they placed her in a special training program designed to cultivate the country's elite athletes.

Under the guidance of her coach, Jutta Müller, Witt's skills blossomed. Her training was rigorous, and her dedication to the sport was unwavering. By age 16, she had already won her country's national championship, a title she would manage to hold onto for the next seven years.

Witt's rise to prominence was marked by her ability to blend athleticism and sheer physical strength with breathtaking artistic expression. Known for her glamorous and creative costume choices, Witt revolutionized the way figure skaters presented themselves, adding an extra layer of artistry to her performances. Katarina dominated international figure skating competitions in the 1980s, winning her first world title in 1984. Her performances were famous for their grace and charm, which captivated audiences and judges alike.

In order to achieve such an original, compelling style on the ice, Witt dedicated countless hours to perfecting her routines. Her training regimen was intense, focusing on both the technical and artistic aspects of figure skating. A constant drive toward perfection helped her develop routines that were as beautiful as they were technically challenging.

Witt's biggest achievements came at the Olympic Games. In 1984, she won her first Olympic gold medal at the Sarajevo Winter Games, narrowly defeating her competitors. She repeated this feat in 1988 in Calgary, becoming the first woman to win consecutive gold medals in Olympic figure skating since Sonja Henie in 1936 (*Katarina Witt*, n.d.-a). Her performances in Calgary, especially her interpretation of the heroine from Bizet's opera *Carmen*, were hailed as being near-perfect routines by spectators and judges alike.

After retiring from amateur skating in 1988, Witt continued to be a well-recognized name in the sport. In recognition of her contributions and achievements, she was inducted into the World Figure Skating Hall of Fame in 1995. This honor confirmed the fact that she was truly one of the greatest figure skaters of the 20th Century.

Katarina's path to success in Olympic figure skating wasn't just about winning medals but also about breaking barriers and setting new standards. Her ability to combine athleticism with artistry set her apart and continues to inspire new generations of skaters for decades to come.

Katarina's story encourages us to challenge stereotypes and strive for equality. She broke barriers in figure skating, not just with her athletic abilities but also by pushing the boundaries of artistic expression. Katarina's journey to the top of the Olympic world reminds us to stand up against stereotypes and fight for equality in all areas of life. By challenging norms and advocating for change, we can create a more inclusive and fairer world.

Her artistic performances on the ice inspire us to be creative and authentic. She brought a unique blend of athleticism and artistry to figure skating, making her routines memorable and impactful. Katarina's story shows us the power of self-expression and encourages us to embrace our creativity. By being true to ourselves and expressing our individuality, we can leave a lasting impression and inspire others with our authenticity.

Witt's achievements inspire us to believe in ourselves and pursue our dreams relentlessly. Her dedication to the sport and ability to overcome challenges serve as a powerful example for us all. Katarina's story encourages us to set lofty goals for ourselves and work tirelessly to achieve them. By believing in ourselves and our abilities, we can inspire others to follow their dreams and reach for the stars just like Katarina did.

KATARINA WITT FUN FACTS

- Katarina had an intense competition with the American skater Debi Thomas at the 1988 games, which was amplified by the political tensions between the U.S. and communist East Germany. This tension was diffused when The Berlin Wall came down just one year later.
- After retiring, Witt became an ambassador for figure skating, inspiring and mentoring young skaters while advocating for physical activity and a healthy lifestyle.
- After retiring from skating, Katarina also built a successful career in television and entertainment, appearing in movies and TV shows, serving as a commentator, and participating in the reality show *Dancing on Ice*.
- Witt has been actively involved in various charitable efforts, including supporting UNICEF and the Special Olympics.
- She has received numerous honors aside from her induction into the Figure Skating Hall of Fame. She has been honored with the Order of Merit of Berlin and is a member of the International Women's Sports Hall of Fame.

THINGS TO THINK ABOUT

- Everyone loved Katarina's skating so much because it was like real dancing on ice. What's your creative outlet, and how can you glide through it with style and grace like Katarina?
- Katarina broke ice-skating stereotypes. Can you think of a time when you challenged norms? How can Katarina's story inspire you to shatter barriers?

- Katarina inspires skaters worldwide. Who's your skating hero, and how can Katarina's moves fire up your own dreams on the ice?

UP NEXT

Since we're gliding gracefully on the ice with Katarina Witt, let's stick with the winter scenery but move from the ice rink to the snowy peaks and thrilling slopes of snowboarding with Chloe Kim! We're going to learn the story of this incredible athlete who redefined what's possible in the world of snowboarding with her groundbreaking performances and inspiring Olympic success story.

Chapter 12

CHLOE KIM

> *The one thing I learned is to just give everything a shot. You don't want to live in regret.*
>
> –CHLOE KIM

At just 17 years old, Chloe Kim soared to the pinnacle of Olympic snowboarding, becoming the youngest woman to have ever won a gold medal in the sport. Her path toward Olympic glory, from being just a little tyke trying out the sport for the first time at age 4 to an international champion, shows us what having a fearless attitude can do.

Chloe's story is about giving everything a shot and living without regret, inspiring young athletes like you to pursue your passions relentlessly.

CHLOE'S STORY

Chloe Kim was born in Long Beach, California, far away from the powder found in Northern California's mountains. But that didn't stop her from becoming the greatest snowboarder of all time.

Chloe's dad took her to the slopes of California's San Gabriel Mountains when she was only four! Just like fellow Olympic snowboarding superstar Shaun White, Chloe was good at snowboarding right away, she had a natural sense of balance and could really fly down the slopes. Recognizing her talent and passion, her parents supported her training, leading her to split time between the U.S. and Switzerland from ages 8 to 10.

In the Swiss Alps, Chloe trained rigorously with the top snowboarding professionals in the world, sharpening her skills and developing a deep connection with the sport.

When she got back to California to start middle school, Chloe joined a developmental snowboarding team, allowing her to show off her skills and start competing. At just 13, she made her debut at the X Games, earning a silver medal in the superpipe competition. She became the youngest competitor ever to get a medal at the X Games. Chloe's early success was just a glimpse into her promising future in the sport.

Despite facing doubts and criticism due to her young age and Asian-American heritage, Chloe persevered against the odds. She continued to impress at the X Games, winning multiple gold medals and establishing herself as a top contender in the sport. Her ability to overcome challenges and rise above naysayers became a significant part of her story. Chloe didn't care what others said. She knew she was great at what she did and would only get better!

Chloe's defining moment came at the 2018 PyeongChang Olympics. At 17, she made history, taking home the gold medal in the halfpipe event. Her first run in the finals received a score of 93.75, putting her in the lead, and she solidified her victory with a nearly perfect score of 98.25 (*Chloe Kim*, n.d.) in her final run. Her performance in the final, including two massive 1080° spins in a row, was simply groundbreaking.

Chloe continued to build on the legacy she'd established, winning yet another gold medal at the 2022 Beijing Olympics. Chloe's first run in the halfpipe finals scored 94 points, far surpassing her competitors. Although she attempted a 1260° spin in her next set of runs, her first run was enough to clinch the gold medal. Chloe Kim's path to snowboarding success shows us the power of intensive training, dedication, and big dreams.

Today, Chloe Kim continues to push the boundaries of snowboarding while balancing her academic pursuits and personal interests. After taking a break from competitive snowboarding to go to Princeton University, Chloe returned to the sport, winning her sixth X Games superpipe gold medal in 2021. Her dedication to snowboarding remains unwavering, and she continues to train rigorously, aiming to compete in future Winter Olympics.

Beyond her athletic career, Chloe has also been a strong advocate for mental health, openly discussing the pressures of competitive sports and the importance of mental well-being. She frequently shares her personal experiences and professional triumphs with fans through social media, sharing insights into her training, personal life, and the causes she supports.

Chloe Kim's influence goes beyond the world of snowboarding too. Today, she's inspiring a new generation of athletes to pursue their passions fearlessly and embrace any challenges that come their way with fearlessness and a positive attitude. By embracing obstacles and persevering through tough times, we can achieve great things and reach new heights.

The confidence Chloe exudes reminds us to trust in our abilities and never doubt ourselves. Despite her young age and the pressures of competing at the highest levels, Chloe believed in her skills and followed her passion. Her story encourages us to have confidence in our talents and to pursue our goals with determination. When we believe in ourselves, we can overcome any challenge and achieve our dreams.

Chloe Kim's resounding success in her sport encourages us to embrace diversity and celebrate our differences. As an Asian-American athlete, she has become a role model for people from diverse backgrounds. Chloe's story shows us that our unique identities and experiences can be our strengths. By celebrating diversity and promoting inclusion, we can create a richer and more inclusive Olympic community where everyone has the opportunity to succeed.

CHLOE KIM FUN FACTS

- Chloe's 2018 Olympic win in the halfpipe event made her the youngest woman to ever win an Olympic gold medal for snowboarding.
- Chloe was named one of TIME's 100 Most Influential People.

THINGS TO THINK ABOUT

- Chloe Kim's achievements inspire young athletes around the world. Who inspires you, and how can Chloe's journey motivate you to pursue your passions relentlessly?
- Chloe broke snowboarding barriers as an Asian-American. How do you celebrate diversity at your school with your classmates? How can Chloe's story inspire you to embrace differences?
- Chloe faced doubters but soared to success. Have you ever proved someone wrong? How did you do it, and what can you learn from Chloe's fearless attitude?

UP NEXT

Chloe Kim's journey from a young snowboarder in Southern California to an Olympic gold medalist exemplifies the power of dedication to the sport, showing how it can give you the power to break barriers. Her story also shows us the power of perseverance and the power found in embracing our ethnic heritage. As Chloe continues to dominate the slopes and advocate for important causes, her standing as the greatest female snowboarder of all time is only further confirmed.

After shredding the slopes with Chloe Kim, it's time to float like a butterfly and sting like a bee with none other than Muhammad Ali!

Chapter 13

MUHAMMAD ALI

66 *He who is not courageous enough to take risks will accomplish nothing in life.*

–MUHAMMAD ALI

Muhammad Ali is still known today as *the* definitive boxing legend of all time. His impact extended far beyond the ring and his words resonated throughout both mainstream culture and the movement for social justice.

Known for his quick wit, unmatched skills, and unwavering defiance in the face of discrimination, Ali became a global icon of courage and determination. This chapter is all about the life of a sports hero who fought epic battles in the ring while standing firm against injustices, inspiring millions worldwide. Let's explore how Ali's relentless spirit and boldness in and outside the ring blazed a path through the sports world.

MUHAMMAD'S STORY

Born in Louisville, Kentucky, Muhammad Ali's birthname was Cassius Marcellus Clay Jr. Growing up in the segregated South, he faced racial prejudice from an early age. Cassius's dad, Cassius Marcellus Clay Sr., painted billboards and signs for a living, while his mother, Odessa Grady Clay, worked as a maid. Money was tight in the Clay family, but despite the challenges and financial hardship they faced, Cassius's parents raised him with a strong sense of pride and determination.

Cassius discovered his love for boxing when he was 12. He used to love riding his bike around; that was until it got stolen. Cassius was really miffed! He wanted to find the guy who did it and get revenge. He couldn't find any information about what happened to the bike, so he went to the police to report it stolen. Down at the precinct, young Cassius Clay told an officer about what happened. As it turned out, the officer whom Cassius talked to that day was, in fact, a boxing coach. His name was Joe Martin. Joe saw a spark in young Cassius's eye. He knew that he had a fighting spirit and that he could teach him to fight. Who knows, maybe one day he'll take boxing seriously, Joe thought.

Cassius went to the gym where Joe trained other boxers and got some lessons. He progressed quickly, fighting his way through the amateur ranks, showing remarkable talent and dedication at training sessions and matches. Cassius had what it takes to go pro, but first, he'd take things to the pinnacle of amateur sports competition at the Olympics!

Heading off to the 1960 Olympics in Rome, Cassius didn't know what to expect. He was going to be competing on the international stage for the first time. He ended up winning a gold medal in the light heavyweight division, an achievement that propelled him into the national spotlight. His victory in Rome was marked by his nimbleness, speed, agility, and confidence. This win wasn't just a personal triumph; it was also a symbolic victory for African Americans during a time of intense racial segregation back home in the United States.

In 1964, Cassius's public profile reached new heights when he became a contender for the heavyweight championship. His opponent was a tough, intimidating boxer named Sonny Liston, and Cassius was definitely the underdog. In a stunning upset, Cassius defeated Liston, proclaiming to the world that he was the greatest of all time. Shortly after this victory, he made a life-changing decision. He announced that he had converted to Islam and had joined the Nation of Islam.

Rejecting what he called his "slave name," he adopted the name Muhammad Ali. This change was a powerful statement of his new identity and beliefs, and it marked a time of great change in his life and career.

With his new name and ideology in place, he became an outspoken advocate for civil rights, using his fame to speak out against racial injustice. His most controversial stance came in 1967 when he refused to be drafted into the Vietnam War, citing his religious beliefs and opposition to the pointless war.

This bold move led to a negative response from the public, which was followed by legal battles and the eventual suspension of his boxing license. Ali even got his world heavyweight title stripped away— just for his anti-war comments! Though he upset many politicians and conservative Americans, his strong stance of resistance made him a hero to countless others.

Ali's refusal to serve in the military got him into a lot of trouble too. It resulted in a conviction for draft evasion, a $10,000 fine (Makin, 2022), and a five-year prison sentence (Piccotti, 2021). Although he remained free on bail during the appeals process, Ali was barred from boxing for three and a half years. His conviction was finally overturned by the Supreme Court in 1971, allowing him to return to the sport he loved.

Ali's return to boxing was marked by his fierce rivalry with "Smokin'" Joe Frazier. The two fighters first clashed in 1971 in what many called the Fight of the Century. Ali lost this match, but he later defeated Frazier in their two subsequent bouts, including the legendary Thrilla in Manila match-up in 1975, which was considered one of the greatest fights in boxing history.

Throughout his career, Ali became the world heavyweight champion three times, a feat unmatched in boxing history. He first claimed the title in 1964 by defeating Sonny Liston, and his victories over Joe Frazier and George Foreman cemented his status as "The Greatest." Ali's charisma, poetic trash talk, and unparalleled skill in the ring captivated audiences worldwide.

In 1974, Ali faced George Foreman in the Rumble in the Jungle, a historic fight held in Zaire (today, the Democratic Republic of the Congo). Using his innovative "rope-a-dope" strategy, Ali absorbed Foreman's powerful punches by leaning against the ropes, allowing Foreman to tire himself out. In the eighth round, Ali launched a successful counterattack, knocking out Foreman and reclaiming the heavyweight title.

Diagnosed with Parkinson's disease at age 42, Ali faced this new challenge with the same courage and determination he showed in the ring. Despite having a condition that affected his ability to move, he continued to make public appearances while also participating in various fundraising and charity initiatives. Ali's contributions to society extended beyond boxing; he was a global ambassador for peace and humanitarian causes.

Although he met much public opposition for his radical ideas, Ali's impact was recognized with numerous awards later in his life, including the Presidential Medal of Freedom in 2005. This honor didn't just celebrate his athletic achievements but recognized his dedication to civil rights and humanitarian efforts. He also received the President's Award from the NAACP in 2009, underscoring his importance as a voice for African Americans all across the nation. Ali's legacy as a champion both in and out of the ring continues to inspire generations.

His life story is one of resilience, bravery, and unwavering belief in justice. His legacy transcends sports, making him a symbol of courage and conviction worldwide. The confidence that he showed in all athletic and social pursuits teaches us to believe in ourselves. He was known for his bold declarations and unwavering self-belief, which played a crucial role in his success both inside and outside the boxing ring. Ali's story encourages us to have faith in our abilities and pursue our dreams with determination and confidence. When we believe in ourselves, we can overcome obstacles and become legendary.

MUHAMMAD ALI FUN FACTS

- Aside from being the greatest boxer of all time, Muhammad Ali was known for his way with words. He often penned his own poems, many of which he used to taunt his opponents before fights. One of his most famous lines is, "Float like a butterfly, sting like a bee. The hands can't hit what the eyes can't see." (Whiteman, 2016).
- One of the most memorable moments in Olympic history took place in 1996 when Ali, despite his battle with Parkinson's, lit the Olympic flame at the opening ceremony of the Atlanta Games.
- Muhammad Ali's life and career have been the subject of numerous films and documentaries, including *When We Were Kings*, which won an Academy Award for Best Documentary Feature, and the biographical film, *Ali*, starring Will Smith.

THINGS TO THINK ABOUT

- Muhammad Ali was fast on his feet! What's your super skill, and how can you zoom through life like a champ?
- Ali stood for what he believed in. When did you stand your ground? How can you fight for what's right like Ali?
- He fought for more than titles. How can you be a hero for others, just like Ali?

UP NEXT

From the boxing ring with Muhammad Ali, whose quick wit and lightning-fast punches electrified the world, we now sprint to the track and field arena with Paavo Nurmi. Just as Ali floated like a butterfly and stung like a bee, Nurmi dominated his sport with unparalleled grace and endurance.

So, get ready to be inspired by another legend who pushed the limits of human potential and redefined what it means to be a champion.

Chapter 14

PAAVO NURMI

66 *Champions are not made in the comfort of their victories, but in the countless hours of hard work and perseverance that lead up to them.*

—PAAVO NURMI

Paavo Nurmi, known as the "Flying Finn," revolutionized the world of middle and long-distance running. Paavo's story is one of relentless dedication and innovative training methods. His path, from being a small rural town to becoming one of the greatest athletes in Olympic history, drives home the power of hard work and dedication.

In this chapter, we'll find out how Nurmi's unconventional training routines, athletic achievements, and unbreakable spirit made him a legend in the world of athletics.

PAAVO'S STORY

Paavo Nurmi was born in Turku, Finland, into a humble rural family. Growing up in a modest environment with nothing but farmlands around, there wasn't much to do. Paavo had to find his own entertainment. This is how he discovered his passion for running early in life, as he'd run through fields of grain and flowers every day. His determination and natural talent for athletics were beginning to emerge. The discipline he'd been developing would eventually lead to a promising career in distance running.

Paavo's rise to the top rungs of international competition began at the 1920 Olympic Games in Antwerp, Belgium. At just age 23, he won his first Olympic medal, gaining gold medals in the 10,000-meter and cross-country individual and team events, as well as a silver in the 5,000-meter. These early achievements were just the beginning though, as he'd later come to dominate long-distance running.

The 1924 Paris Olympics solidified Nurmi's legendary status. In an extraordinary display of endurance and skill, he won five gold medals in just four days. His victories included the 1,500-meter, 5,000-meter, and 3,000-meter team events and two different cross-country events. This unbelievable performance made him the first athlete to win five gold medals at a single Olympic Games (IOC, 2016).

Beyond the Olympics, Nurmi's influence on middle-distance running became legendary. He set multiple world records in events including the 1,500 meters and the mile. His strategic approach to running, often carrying a stopwatch to properly regulate his pace, revolutionized training and racing techniques. On August 23, 1923, he set a world record for the mile with a time of 4 minutes and 10.4 seconds, a record that stood for eight years before being broken (*Paavo Nurmi*, n.d.).

Nurmi's success attracted global attention, and he was invited to compete in athletic meets worldwide. This widespread popularity, however, led to controversy. In 1932, the International Amateur Athletic Federation (IAAF) declared that he was a professional, effectively ending his amateur career and barring him from competing in the 1932 Olympics. This decision cost him a potential 10th gold medal he could have won had the policy been more lax.

Paavo's story shows us the power of disciplined training regimens and innovation in sports. His unconventional training methods, constant pursuit of excellence, and ability to overcome obstacles made him a trailblazer in athletics. His legacy continues to inspire athletes around the world to push the boundaries of what is possible. His career achievements and influence on the sport remain a significant part of Olympic history, showing us the impact of hard work, determination, and strategic thinking in achieving greatness.

The sheer perseverance Paavo showed teaches us to never give up. Despite facing numerous challenges throughout his career, Nurmi continued to push forward and strive for greatness. His relentless determination made him one of the greatest distance runners in Olympic history. Nurmi's story reminds us that persistence is key to overcoming obstacles and achieving our goals. By continuing to move forward, even when the going gets tough, we can reach new heights and accomplish amazing things.

Paavo's dedication shows that hard work pays off. He trained tirelessly, developing innovative techniques and strategies that set him apart from his competitors. His self-belief inspires us to believe in ourselves. He had confidence in his abilities and training, which allowed him to perform at his best and achieve remarkable success. Nurmi's story encourages us to have faith in our own potential and pursue our goals with confidence.

PAAVO NURMI FUN FACTS

- As part of his intensive training, Paavo often ran up to 35 miles a day, a practice considered a bit extreme at the time.
- Paavo developed the "Nurmi Technique," a running that involved taking smaller, quicker strides to maximize efficiency and minimize any wasted energy. His technique was later adopted by other runners, fundamentally changing middle-distance races.

- Throughout his career, Nurmi set an astounding 22 world records across various distances, from 1500 meters to 20 kilometers (*30 Best Paavo Nurmi Quotes with Image*, n.d.).

THINGS TO THINK ABOUT

- Paavo trained really hard. How do you practice? How can you use this as inspiration to get better and more disciplined in the sports you love to play?
- Nurmi loved to win! Do you enjoy competing? How do you handle victory and defeat, and what can you learn from Nurmi's competitive spirit?
- Nurmi faced hurdles but kept running. Ever faced an obstacle? How did you overcome it, and what can you learn from Nurmi's determination?

UP NEXT

From the hot sun-beaten track with Paavo Nurmi to the ice rink's cold air, let's switch gears from the Summer to the Winter Olympics for some thrilling winter sports action.

Get ready to learn about the story of Eric Heiden, whose speed and endurance on ice brought him legendary status in speed skating. You're sure to be inspired by his dedication, training, and sheer willpower that led him to dominate the ice.

Chapter 15

ERIC HEIDEN

> 66 *It is not the events in our life that define our character, but how we deal with them.*
>
> *—ERIC HEIDEN*

Eric Heiden's path to success on the ice is a lesson in versatility and determination. His athletic career is marked by incredible achievements across multiple sports, demonstrating that true greatness comes from pushing boundaries and never settling for a single path. Heiden's journey from a young skater in Wisconsin to a celebrated Olympic champion and respected orthopedic surgeon shows that success is about embracing challenges and continually striving for excellence.

In this chapter, we'll be tracing his life, highlighting how his diverse talents and relentless drive made him an enduring inspiration.

ERIC'S STORY

Born in Madison, Wisconsin, Eric Heiden's journey into the world of sports began almost as soon as he could walk. Growing up in a family that valued physical activity and sports, Eric was encouraged to explore various athletic pursuits from a young age. His natural talent and determination became evident early on, as he began skating shortly after he learned to walk.

Eric grew up just like any other kid; he played outside a lot. Eric's dad, Jack, was a doctor and professor, and his mother, Nancy, was a high school teacher—both supported and nurtured their children's athletic ambitions. Eric, along with his younger sister Beth, who would also grow up to become a world-class speed skater, spent countless hours on the ice, developing their skills and building their strength. The Heiden siblings often skated at local rinks and practiced relentlessly, driven by a shared passion for the sport.

Eric's early training was rigorous and multifaceted. He combined traditional skating practice with running, bicycling, and weightlifting, setting a foundation for his incredible endurance and strength. By the time he was a teenager, Eric's dedication and hard work began to pay off, and he started to gain recognition for his exceptional abilities on the ice.

Eric was never content just being good at one sport. In addition to his mastery of speed skating, he is also a very accomplished cyclist. Heiden's versatility as an athlete was amazing; he managed to compete at a high level in both sports simultaneously. His commitment to maintaining peak physical condition and his relentless training regimen allowed him to excel at both of these demanding sports at the same time.

Heiden's best achievements yet came during the 1980 Winter Olympics, which took place in Lake Placid, New York. At just 21 years old, he managed to achieve one of the most remarkable feats in Olympic history by winning five gold medals in speed skating. He swept all the men's events from 500 meters to 10,000 meters, setting an Olympic record in each race and a world record in the 10,000-meter event. His performance in Lake Placid firmed up his status as one of the greatest speed skaters of all time.

After his success in speed skating, Heiden turned his attention to professional cycling. He quickly proved that his talents extended beyond the ice rink. In 1985, he won the US Professional Cycling Championship, proving that he had what it took to compete in both sports. He also competed in the prestigious Tour de France in 1986, further solidifying his reputation as a multi-sport athlete.

Eric Heiden's achievements weren't limited to the realm of sports. Following his retirement from competitive athletics, he followed in his dad's footsteps and pursued a career in medicine. Eric went off to Stanford University where he earned an MD and went on to become an orthopedic surgeon, giving him a chance to help other athletes with sports injuries. His focus on sports medicine allowed him to combine his passion for sports with his medical expertise, helping other athletes achieve their best.

Eric Heiden's success in multiple sports teaches us the value of versatility. His story encourages us to explore different interests and try new activities. By being versatile and open to various opportunities, we can discover our strengths and find success in multiple areas.

Eric's intense concentration under pressure reminds us to stay focused on our goals. During his remarkable performances at the Winter Olympics, Heiden maintained his composure and delivered outstanding results. His ability to stay focused, even in high-pressure situations, was key to his success. Heiden's story shows us the importance of maintaining our concentration and not getting distracted, especially when it matters most.

Eric's dedication to training highlights the importance of hard work. He put in countless hours of rigorous training to reach the pinnacle of his sport. His commitment to his craft and relentless work ethic were crucial to his achievements. His story inspires us to put in the effort and stay disciplined in our pursuits. By working hard and staying dedicated, we can achieve our dreams and excel in whatever we set out to do.

ERIC HEIDEN FUN FACTS

- At the peak of Eric's intensive training, his thighs measured an astounding 29 inches in circumference (Furman, 2006).
- Heiden still holds the record for the highest measure ever recorded on the "Wingate" test, a test that measures a skater's power.

THINGS TO THINK ABOUT

- Eric trained really hard to reach the top. What's your favorite way to train or practice? How can you train like Eric did to improve in your favorite activity?
- Have you ever felt pressure to perform on the spot or in front of an audience? How did you handle it, and what can you learn from Eric's ability to stay cool under pressure?
- Eric was a great skater and cyclist. Do you enjoy trying different activities? How can you embrace your versatility and explore new interests just like Heiden did?

UP NEXT

Let's stay out on the ice and glide from one legendary speedskater to another! Eric Heiden's incredible sports career has shown us the limitless possibilities of athletic dedication and versatility. Now, let's get ready to be inspired by another skating icon, Bonnie Blair. With her top-gear speed and fierce determination, Bonnie dominated the ice and left a big mark on the history of the Winter Olympics. So, lace up your skates and get ready to meet the phenomenal Bonnie Blair.

Chapter 16

BONNIE BLAIR

" *Winning doesn't always mean being first. Winning means you're doing better than you've ever done before.*

–BONNIE BLAIR

Bonnie Blair's story is a great example of what it means to push beyond your limits and redefine success. From her early days on the ice to her record-breaking performances at the Winter Olympics, Bonnie's path to speedskating success has been one of relentless determination and passion. Her incredible achievements in the sport have made her an inspiration for athletes worldwide.

This chapter is all about the life of Bonnie Blair. We'll learn how, through hard work, dedication, and talent, she became one of the greatest speed skaters in history.

BONNIE'S STORY

Bonnie Blair was born in Cornwall, New York, into a family that was passionate about skating. Her parents, Charles and Eleanor, encouraged all their children to skate every winter when the ponds froze over, creating an atmosphere where the love for the sport was nurtured from a young age. Bonnie learned how to skate almost as soon as she could walk, and by the time she was just four years old, she was already entering races. Her family moved to Champaign, Illinois, a hub for speed-skating training, where she'd have top-notch coaching and rigorous competition opportunities.

Bonnie's natural talent for speed skating was evident early on. At 15, her coach introduced her to an Olympic-style competition, where skaters raced against the clock in pairs. Her amazing speed and technical skating skills quickly became apparent, and within just two years, she was competing internationally. At the 1984 Winter Olympics in Sarajevo, she came in eighth place in the 500-meter event, marking the beginning of what would come to be a long Olympic saga.

Bonnie's rise to prominence continued at the 1988 Winter Olympics in Calgary. It was there that she won her first gold medal in the 500-meter event, setting a new world record with a finish time of 39.10 seconds (*Bonnie Blair*, 2024). At those same games, she also earned a bronze medal in the 1,000-meter event. Her performance in Calgary established her as a real competitor on the world stage.

The pinnacle of Bonnie's career came in the following years. In the 1992 Olympics in Albertville, France, she defended her 500-meter title and won another gold in the 1,000-meter event. In the 1994 Winter Olympics in Lillehammer, Norway, she repeated this incredible feat, winning gold medals in both the 500-meter and 1,000-meter events. Her victory margins in these races were significant, particularly in the 1,000-meter event in Lillehammer, where she won by 1.38 seconds (*Bonnie Blair*, 2020), the largest margin in the event's history!

Bonnie's technique was what drove her success and domination of the sport. Despite having a small stature, Bonnie's technique was nearly flawless. She maintained an accentuated crouch and a smooth rhythm throughout her races, which allowed her to sustain speed and efficiency, outpacing her competitors who often faltered due to technical inconsistencies.

Throughout her career, Blair accumulated numerous awards and recognitions. She received the Sportswoman of the Year award from the U.S. Olympic Committee in 1992 and 1994, and in between these recognitions, she received the 1993 James E. Sullivan Award as the top amateur athlete in the country. In 1994, her Sportswoman of the Year title echoed with similar recognitions from *Sports Illustrated*, the Women's Sports Foundation, and the Babe Zaharias Foundation.

After retiring from competitive skating on her 31st birthday, Bonnie transitioned to a new role as a motivational speaker and charity advocate. Her story continues to inspire young athletes and those who strive for excellence in their pursuits, demonstrating the power of hard work, dedication, and a supportive family.

Bonnie Blair's Olympic triumphs remind us to celebrate our accomplishments and the milestones we achieve along the path to eventual success. Her numerous gold medals and world records are a testament to her hard work and dedication. Bonnie's story encourages us to take pride in our successes, no matter how big or small, and to acknowledge the progress we make. By celebrating our achievements, we can stay motivated and inspired to continue striving for our goals.

Bonnie's teamwork and support from her coaches and teammates highlight the importance of surrounding ourselves with a supportive network of people who believe in us. Her success was not just a solo effort but a result of the encouragement and guidance she received from those around her. Her story teaches us the value of building a strong support system and being there for others as they pursue their dreams. Together, we can achieve more and lift each other up.

Bonnie's dedication to inspiring others shows us the importance of giving back to our communities and using our platforms to make a positive impact on the lives of others. She has been involved in various charitable activities and has worked to motivate young athletes. Bonnie's story encourages us to use our talents and achievements to help others and contribute to the well-being of our communities. By giving back, we can create a ripple effect of positivity and make a lasting difference.

BONNIE BLAIR FUN FACTS

- When she was honored with the prestigious James E. Sullivan Award in 1993, Bonnie was only the third winter athlete to have ever won it. She was also the only female speed skater to have ever been granted the honor.
- Bonnie was one of the final torchbearers to carry the Olympic flame during the opening ceremony of the 2002 Winter Olympics in Salt Lake City, Utah.
- Bonnie currently serves on the board of The Pettit National Ice Center in Milwaukee, Wisconsin, and is actively present in the sport despite being retired.

THINGS TO THINK ABOUT

- Do you enjoy competition? How do you handle winning and losing, and what can you learn from Blair's competitive drive?
- What's a personal record you'd like to achieve, and how can you work toward it with determination, just like Blair did?
- Despite setbacks, Blair kept striving for success. How do you stay motivated when faced with challenges, and what can you learn from Blair's determination to never give up?

UP NEXT

As we transition from the world of speed skating with Bonnie Blair, let's stay on the ice but move on to a different sport. That's right! We're going straight into the graceful and exhilarating realm of figure skating. Get ready to meet Yuna Kim, an athlete whose elegance, precision, and artistry have not only earned her a place among the greats but also captivated audiences worldwide.

Known as "Queen Yuna," she has left an indelible mark on the sport with her record-breaking performances and iconic routines. Let's learn the story of Yuna Kim and find out how she rose up to become a global icon in figure skating.

Chapter 17

YUNA KIM

> *Even in the hardest circumstances, dreams can give you the courage to live, and I hope I can share that message with children in need.*
>
> —YUNA KIM

Yuna Kim's path to figure skating fame, from a young girl in South Korea to a global figure skating icon is nothing short of inspiring. Her story is one of being relentlessly dedicated, overcoming challenges, and achieving greatness on the world stage.

From her early introduction to skating at age 6 to her historic performances at the Winter Olympics, Yuna's story teaches us the power of dreams and hard work. As we explore her captivating career, we'll discover how she became South Korea's beloved figure skater and an inspiration to millions worldwide.

YUNA'S STORY

Yuna Kim was born in Bucheon, South Korea. From a very young age, she showed an affinity for the ice. Encouraged by her mother, she started figure skating at age 6. This early start laid the foundation for what would become an illustrious career in figure skating.

Kim's entry into the competitive figure skating world was swift and successful. At just age 12, she began competing internationally, quickly making a name for herself. In 2002, she won the novice-level Triglav Trophy competition in Jesenice, Slovenia. Her success continued as she captured her first South Korean national title in 2003.

Demonstrating remarkable talent and dedication, she entered the Junior Grand Prix circuit the following year, securing gold in Hungary and winning in the Final competition of the Junior Grand Prix, which took place in the Czech Republic. Kim's crowning achievement at the junior level came in 2006 when she took home the gold medal at the World Junior Championships.

The transition from junior to senior level can be challenging for many young skaters, but Yuna handled it with grace and excellence making her a star back home. In the 2006–07 season, she took home the title at the Grand Prix Finals in both 2006 and 2007 and clinched a bronze medal at the 2007 World Championships. Recognizing the need for advanced training, Kim moved to Canada to work with Brian Orser, a two-time Olympic silver medalist. This move was instrumental in refining her skills and preparing her for the highest levels of competition.

In 2009, Kim made history at the World Championships by becoming the first South Korean to win a world figure skating title at the senior level. She achieved a record-breaking score of 207.71 points (DiGiacomo, 2018), surpassing the previous mark set by her rival Mao Asada of Japan. Kim's performances throughout the 2009 season, including victories at two Grand Prix competitions and the Grand Prix final, established her as the favorite for the 2010 Winter Olympics in Vancouver.

At the 2010 Winter Olympics, Yuna Kim delivered a performance that would go down in history. Her nearly flawless routine, which featured seven triple jumps, earned her a gold medal and a world record score of 228.56 points, more than 23 points over the score of the second-best competitor, beating the previously held record by 8.19 points (*Kim Yuna*, 2020). This victory was monumental for Kim and South Korea, as it was the nation's first Olympic gold medal in a sport other than speed skating.

Following her Olympic triumph, Kim continued to compete at the highest levels. She won silver medals at the 2010 and 2011 World Championships before taking a hiatus from competitive skating. During her break, Kim stayed in the public eye in her home country and was chosen to serve as an ambassador for South Korea's successful bid to host the 2018 Winter Olympics in Pyeongchang. She returned to professional competition in 2013, winning her second World Championship title by a big margin.

In the 2014 Winter Olympics in Sochi, Kim was once again the favorite to win gold. Her performances were exceptional, but she was narrowly edged out by Russia's Adelina Sotnikova, who ended up taking the gold medal. Kim's elegant and technically impeccable routines earned her a well-deserved silver medal though, adding to her impressive Olympic legacy. Despite the unexpected outcome, Kim's grace and sportsmanship shone through, and she was celebrated globally for her outstanding contributions to figure skating.

After the 2014 Olympics, Kim announced her retirement from competitive skating. She shifted her focus to other pursuits, including serving as a spokeswoman for various causes and continuing to promote sports in South Korea.

One of the defining features of Yuna's skating is her ability to convey deep emotion and tell a story through her performances. Her routines are known for their elegance and artistic expression, making her a favorite among fans and judges alike.

Throughout her career, Yuna's accomplishments have extended far beyond her Olympic medals. Her unique combination of technical mastery and artistic expression set her apart from her peers, making her routines memorable and inspiring for both fans and aspiring skaters.

Yuna also made headlines for her philanthropic efforts. She has been involved in numerous charitable activities, particularly focusing on supporting young athletes and children in need, serving as a UNICEF Goodwill Ambassador. Yuna's dedication to giving back to the community further solidified her status as a beloved figure both in South Korea and internationally.

Today, Yuna remains a prominent cultural icon in South Korea. She has been featured in various media campaigns, endorsing products and brands, and has remained an important part of the country's popular culture. Her influence has transcended sports, making her a role model for many young people.

Yuna's story shows us that challenges are opportunities to grow stronger and improve. By embracing difficult situations and persevering through tough times, we can achieve our goals and become the best version of ourselves.

The confidence that Yuna exudes reminds us to trust in our abilities and never doubt ourselves. Despite facing intense competition and the pressure of performing on the world stage, Yuna believed in her skills and remained focused on her dreams. Her journey encourages us to have confidence in our talents and pursue our aspirations with determination. When we believe in ourselves, we can overcome any obstacles and achieve greatness.

YUNA KIM FUN FACTS

- Yuna was the first South Korean figure skater to have ever won a gold medal at the Olympics.

- She is known for her signature move, called the Yuna Kim Spin.
- Yuna was named one of TIME magazine's 100 most influential people.
- Yuna has been inducted into the World Figure Skating Hall of Fame.

THINGS TO THINK ABOUT

- Yuna Kim sparkled under the spotlight. How do you handle the heat, and what can you learn from Kim's cool performance?
- She practiced hard for her performances. What's your favorite hobby, and how can you practice like Kim to shine?
- Yuna became a cultural icon. How do you use your talents to inspire others, and what can you learn from her influence?

UP NEXT

Yuna Kim's legacy is one of excellence, perseverance, and inspiration. She has left a deep mark on the world of figure skating and continues to inspire future generations of athletes with her story of dedication and success.

From twirls on ice to lightning-fast sprints, it's now time to go from the graceful art of figure skating to the electrifying world of track and field. Get ready to meet Wilma Rudolph, a trailblazing sprinter whose speed and determination broke barriers and set new standards in athletics.

Chapter 18

WILMA RUDOLPH

66 *Never underestimate the power of dreams and the influence of the human spirit. We are all the same in this notion: The potential for greatness lives within each of us.*

–WILMA RUDOLPH

Wilma Rudolph's journey from a fragile, sickly child to an Olympic champion is one of the most inspirational stories in all sports history. Wilma faced tremendous challenges in life that could have easily thwarted her dreams. However, her unyielding determination and the support of her family and community helped her overcome these obstacles.

This chapter is all about the life of Wilma Rudolph, highlighting how her dreams and relentless spirit enabled her to defy the odds and win multiple gold medals, becoming a role model and inspiration for generations to come.

WILMA'S STORY

Born prematurely in St. Bethlehem, Tennessee, Wilma faced numerous health challenges from a young age. As one of 22 children, it would have been easy to feel ignored, but instead, she was constantly surrounded by her family's support and care. Wilma was stricken with polio and scarlet fever, and her left leg was paralyzed. She had to wear a leg brace and was told she would never walk again. However, her mother believed otherwise and so did Wilma. With her family's unwavering support, especially through massages for her leg, Wilma began to hop on one leg at age 6 and eventually walked with a leg brace by age 8. Doctors had grave concerns that she might never be able to walk, but with her family's help, she continually massaged her leg and eventually, the brace came off!

Wilma's determination to walk evolved into a passion for sports. By age 11, she discarded her brace and was spotted playing basketball. Her athletic talent became apparent, and she became a high school basketball star, earning All-American honors. It was during a chance meeting with a college track coach that Wilma's path shifted toward track and field. She joined Tennessee State University's track team and started competing at a collegiate level while still in high school.

Wilma Rudolph's athletic talents led her to the 1956 Olympics in Melbourne at just 16. There, she won a bronze medal in the 4x100-meter relay, the first American woman to do so. But it was at the 1960 Rome Olympics that she truly made history. She became the first American woman to win three gold medals in a single Olympics, winning the 100-meter dash, the 200-meter dash, and the 4x100-meter relay. Her victory in the 100-meter dash tied the world record at 11.3 seconds (*Wilma Rudolph*, 2018). In the 200-meter dash, she set a new Olympic record with a time of 23.2 seconds. The 4x100-meter relay team also set a world record of 44.4 seconds (*Wilma Rudolph*, 2018) in a semifinal race, solidifying Rudolph's status as an athletic legend.

Rudolph's performances in Rome weren't just about winning medals; they were ways for her to show off her fluid running style to the world, fundamentally changing how other runners approached the sport. She became a media darling and an inspiration to many, especially African Americans and women, who saw her achievements as breaking barriers and paving the way for future generations.

After her triumphant Olympic career, Rudolph received numerous praises. She was honored with the Associated Press Female Athlete of the Year in 1960 and 1961. She also won the prestigious Sullivan amateur-athlete-of-the-year award in 1961.

In 1974, Wilma was inducted into the National Track and Field Hall of Fame, followed by her induction into the International Sports Hall of Fame in 1980 and the U.S. Olympic Hall of Fame in 1983. Her autobiography, *Wilma*, published in 1977, and a prime-time television movie about her life, brought her story to an even wider audience.

In the years following her retirement from professional competition, Wilma remained committed to the sport and her community. She graduated from Tennessee State University and took on roles that allowed her to influence and mentor young athletes. As an assistant director for a youth foundation in Chicago, she worked to develop track-and-field programs for girls, sharing her knowledge and passion for athletics.

Wilma Rudolph's legacy extends beyond her athletic achievements. She was a trailblazer for civil rights and an advocate for racial equality. Her insistence on a racially integrated homecoming parade and her work in community centers across the United States reflect her commitment to using her platform for social change. In 1990, she became the first woman to receive the NCAA's Silver Anniversary Award, recognizing her significant impact on sports and society.

Wilma Rudolph passed away on November 12, 1994, from a brain tumor, but her legacy lives on. She remains an enduring symbol of courage, perseverance, and the potential for greatness that resides in each of us. Her story continues to inspire athletes and non-athletes alike to pursue their dreams and overcome any obstacles they may face.

Throughout her life and Olympic career, Wilma Rudolph was a symbol of resilience and determination. Her legacy continues to inspire athletes around the world, demonstrating that with perseverance and hard work, it is possible to overcome any obstacle and achieve greatness.

Rudolph's legacy is still celebrated today through various commemorations, including a bronze statue in Clarksville, Tennessee, the Wilma Rudolph Event Center, and a high school in Berlin named after her. June 23 is also celebrated as Wilma Rudolph Day in Tennessee, honoring her contributions to sports and society.

Wilma Rudolph teaches us to never give up no matter what obstacles we face. Despite being told she would never walk again due to polio, Wilma's determination and perseverance led her to become the fastest woman in the world. Her journey reminds us that no matter how tough things get, we can achieve our dreams if we keep going and never lose hope.

Her resilience teaches us to see challenges as opportunities for growth and empowerment. She overcame severe health issues and discrimination to become an Olympic champion. Wilma's story shows us that the challenges we face can make us stronger and more determined. By turning our obstacles into strengths, we can achieve extraordinary things.

Wilma's advocacy for civil rights inspires us to use our talents to make a positive impact in the world. After achieving success on the track, she dedicated herself to fighting for equality and justice. Wilma's story encourages us to use our skills and achievements to inspire change and make a difference in our communities. By standing up for what is right, we can help create a better world for everyone.

WILMA RUDOLPH FUN FACTS

- Legendary boxer Muhammad Ali, then known as Cassius Clay, befriended Rudolph during the 1960 Olympics.
- When Rudolph met President John F. Kennedy in 1961, he was so excited that he fell out of his rocking chair.
- In 1963, Rudolph traveled to West Africa as a cultural ambassador for the U.S. State Department, visiting countries like Senegal, Mali, Guinea, and the Republic of Upper Volta (now Burkina Faso). Her visits helped promote sports and cultural exchange between the U.S. and African nations.

THINGS TO THINK ABOUT

- When things get tough, how do you keep going, and what can you learn from Wilma's determination?
- How can you use your talents to make a difference, like Wilma did both on and off the track?
- What challenges have you faced, and how can you jump over them like Wilma did?

UP NEXT

Get ready to swap your running shoes for cross-country skis as we meet our next Olympic champion: Marit Bjørgen! This legendary athlete has slid her way into the history books with her incredible endurance, strength, and sheer determination.

Let's slide into the frosty world of winter sports and discover how Marit Bjørgen became the queen of the cross-country trails.

Chapter 19

MARIT BJØRGEN

66 *If the motivation is gone, then I am finished.*

−MARIT BJORGEN

Marit Bjørgen's journey from a young skier amid the snowy landscapes of Norway to becoming the most decorated Winter Olympian is a story of unparalleled dedication and resilience. With a legendary career that spans over two decades, Bjørgen has become a symbol of excellence in cross-country skiing. Her ability to overcome setbacks and maintain unwavering motivation has set her apart as a true legend in winter sports.

Let's explore the life story of Marit Bjørgen, from her early days on the slopes to her record-breaking performances on the world stage.

MARIT'S STORY

Marit Bjørgen was born in Trondheim, Norway. She grew up in Rognes, a small village where cross-country skiing is a means of transportation and part of daily life throughout winter. As such, Marit was naturally drawn to the sport, and it suited her. She was quick and well-balanced from a young age.

The snowy landscapes of Norway provided the perfect playground for young Marit, who started skiing almost as soon as she could walk.

By age 7, she was already competing in local races, demonstrating her talent and determination from an early age.

Bjørgen's competitive spirit and skill set her apart from her peers. She made a big impression on the skiing world at age 19, debuting in the World Cup in 1999. Her initial performances were promising, and it was clear that she had the potential to become one of the greats. Over the next few years, she honed her skills and steadily climbed the ranks, establishing herself as a formidable competitor in the World Cup circuit.

Marit's journey through the World Cup was marked by steady progress and increasing success. She secured her first overall World Cup title in the 2004–05 season, a well-deserved recognition of all her hard work and dedication. She continued to dominate the World Cup in the following seasons, winning the overall title again in 2005–06 and 2011–12. Marit's consistency and ability to perform under pressure made her a standout athlete in the world of cross-country skiing.

Bjørgen's success at skiing extended beyond the World Cup as she amassed an impressive collection of World Championship titles. She won her first World Championship gold medal in the individual sprint at the 2003 World Championships in Val di Fiemme. Over her career, she accumulated eighteen World Championship gold medals, twelve of which were individual titles. This record underscores her versatility and excellence in both individual and team events.

Marit Bjørgen's Olympic journey began at the 2002 Games in Salt Lake City. It was there that she won a silver medal in the 4×5-kilometer relay. Despite facing challenges and setbacks in subsequent Olympics events, she persevered.

Her breakthrough came at the 2010 Vancouver Winter Olympics, where she won five medals, including three golds, firmly establishing her as one of the top athletes in her sport.

Marit was doing a great job, but there was just one problem. Like many endurance athletes, she suffered from asthma, a condition that affects breathing, especially during intense physical exertion in cold weather. To manage her condition, she was prescribed a medication that contained substances, like Symbicort, that appeared on the World Anti-Doping Agency (WADA) banned substances list. However, Marit got approval from the International Ski Federation to use it anyway.

Justyna Kowalczyk, a Polish cross-country skier and one of Bjørgen's main rivals, publicly criticized Marit's use of asthma medication. She accused her of having an unfair advantage, implying that the medication could enhance her performance beyond simply managing her asthma symptoms. This accusation sparked widespread public debate and media coverage across the sports world, putting Bjørgen's integrity and regulatory policies under scrutiny.

In September 2011, WADA revised its regulations, allowing the use of Symbicort without a special exemption, provided it is used within prescribed doses. This change acknowledged the medical necessity for many athletes while aiming to maintain a level playing field.

Marit left the incident behind her now vindicated and continued to excel at the 2014 Sochi Olympics and the 2018 Pyeongchang Olympics. By the end of her career, Bjørgen had the most medals of any Winter Olympian ever, having received 15 medals in total, including 8 golds (*Marit Bjoergen*, n.d.).

After retiring from competitive skiing in 2018, Bjørgen's love for the sport led her to join Team Ragde Charge in 2020, focusing on long-distance races like the Vasaloppet. However, after two years, she decided to retire again, citing a lack of motivation. Her decision to step away from the sport was not easy, but it was made with the same thoughtful consideration that characterized her approach to her career.

Marit's story is one of dedication, hard work, and unparalleled success. Her path from a young skier in Norway to the most decorated Winter Olympian of all time shows us how dedication, passion, and beating the odds really can lead to success. Her skiing career continues to inspire athletes around the world, proving that anything is possible with determination and hard work.

Marit's Olympic wins show us the power of setting lofty goals and working hard to achieve them. She dreamed of becoming the best in cross-country skiing and turned that dream into reality with her numerous Olympic medals. Marit's story encourages us to aim high and pursue our passions with determination. By dreaming big and working diligently, we can achieve our greatest aspirations.

Her ability to overcome setbacks reminds us to tackle challenges head-on and grow from them. Throughout her career, she faced injuries and tough competition, but she never let these obstacles deter her. Instead, she used them as motivation to improve and come back stronger. Marit's resilience teaches us to embrace challenges and view them as opportunities for growth and development.

Marit's dedication to training highlights the importance of putting in the effort to succeed. Her rigorous training regimen and an unwavering commitment to the sport were key to her incredible success. Marit's story shows us that hard work and perseverance are essential for achieving our goals. By putting in the time and effort, we can reach new heights and excel in our endeavors.

MARIT BJØRGEN FUN FACTS

- Marit's 15 Olympic medals include 8 gold, 4 silver, and 3 bronzes (*Olympic Legend Bjoergen Reveals the Secrets Behind Her Record-Breaking Career*, 2020). She achieved this incredible feat across five Olympic Games.

- Bjørgen's training involved an average of 940 hours per year during her most successful period from 2010 to 2015. Most of her training was low intensity though, focusing on endurance (Bazilchuk, 2018).

THINGS TO THINK ABOUT

- What about Marit Bjørgen's story inspires you most to hit the slopes?
- What's the most thrilling skiing or snowboarding moment you've had, and how can you create more exciting moments like Marit's victories?
- How do you make skiing or snowboarding feel like a fun adventure, just like Marit?

UP NEXT

Now, it's time to trade out our cross-country ski boots for sprinter spikes as we dash to the speedy track with Lauryn Williams! Get ready to meet an athlete who has made history both on the track and on the ice, showing amazing levels of versatility and determination in her pursuit of excellence.

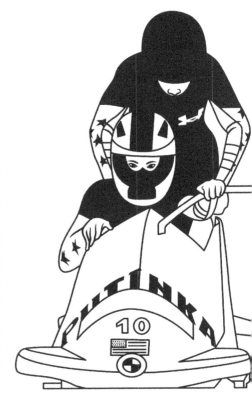

Chapter 20

LAURYN WILLIAMS

> 66 *I had no idea what was in store for me this season. This is the first time I've been a part of a true team sport, and there's someone else counting on you. You can't let that person down, and that's what drives me.*
> –LAURYN WILLIAMS

Lauryn Williams's athletic journey is a tale of triumph against the odds. As both a sprinter and a bobsledder, she achieved a feat that very few athletes in history have accomplished—winning medals in both the Summer and Winter Olympic Games.

Full of drive and determination that comes from teamwork, Lauryn is a truly exemplary athlete. In this chapter, we'll learn Lauryn's remarkable story, from her early days on the track to her groundbreaking achievements on the icy slopes of the bobsled track. Lauryn's journey isn't just about the medals she won; it's also about the power of belief and that of adapting to new challenges. So, let's learn the incredible story of Lauryn Williams, a true icon of versatility and perseverance in the world of sports.

LAURYN'S STORY

Lauryn Williams was born in Rochester, Pennsylvania. From a young age, she showed exceptional athletic talent, particularly in track and field. Her journey into athletics began in fourth grade when she started running track, often competing against boys and easily beating them thanks to her remarkable speed. Her parents recognized her potential and provided unwavering support, encouraging her to pursue her passion for running seriously. Despite her initial shyness, Lauryn's determination and passion for track and field became evident as she progressed through high school and into college.

Lauryn attended the University of Miami, where her athletic prowess truly began to shine. During her junior year in 2004, she became the NCAA Champion in the 100-meter race, clocking the fastest legal wind time by an American that year at 10.97 seconds (*Who I Am*, n.d.). This achievement marked her as the second-fastest sprinter globally in 2004. Her success on the collegiate level translated into international acclaim, where she won gold and silver medals at the World Championships between 2005 and 2007. Her victories in these championships solidified her reputation as a top contender in the world of sprinting events.

Lauryn's Olympic journey began in 2004 at the Athens Games, where she earned a silver medal in the 100-meter race, recording an impressive 10.96 seconds, just behind Yulia Nesterenko of Belarus (*Lauryn Williams*, n.d.). She continued to compete at the highest levels, reaching the finals in the 100-meter race at the 2008 Beijing Games. Her perseverance and dedication culminated in a gold medal in the 4x100-meter relay at the 2012 London Games, cementing her legacy as an Olympic champion.

In 2013, Lauryn faced a significant setback due to a nagging injury that ended her track season prematurely. Uncertain about her future in athletics, she had to think hard about her next steps. This period of uncertainty, however, did not mark the end of her athletic career but rather the beginning of a new chapter. A chance encounter with Olympic hurdler Lolo Jones introduced her to the world of bobsledding, sparking a new athletic direction.

Curious about the opportunity, Lauryn decided to give bobsledding a try. Despite having only one training session and dealing with an injured leg, she competed in the Push Championships in Calgary and finished third, showcasing her adaptability and athleticism. Her rapid ascent in bobsledding led her to join the World Cup Race Circuit in December 2013, where she won two silver medals and one gold in four races. Her exceptional performance earned her a spot on the USA Olympic Bobsled Team for the 2014 Sochi Winter Games.

Unlike track and field, bobsledding required Lauryn to find alternative ways to fund her participation. She sold T-shirts and had to ask people for donations to cover her bobsledding expenses.

Paired with driver Elana Meyers, Lauryn won a silver medal in the two-woman bobsled event, finishing just 0.10 seconds behind the gold medalists (*Lauryn Williams*, n.d.). This achievement made her the first American woman to have won medals in both the Summer and Winter Games, an extraordinary feat!

After her historic bobsledding career, Lauryn transitioned to a new role as a financial planner, launching her business, *Worth Winning*. She also pursued further education, earning a Master of Business Administration degree. Lauryn continues to inspire others through her work as a motivational speaker, podcaster, and advocate for financial literacy among athletes. She balances her personal life with her professional endeavors, demonstrating the same dedication and resilience that marked her athletic career.

Lauryn is also actively involved in community outreach. She contributes to the USA Track and Field's "Be a Champion" program, helping to inspire and support young athletes across the country.

Lauryn Williams's journey from track to bobsled exemplifies versatility, resilience, and a relentless pursuit of excellence. Her story inspires us to embrace new challenges and remain adaptable, proving that with determination and a willingness to explore new avenues, amazing achievements are possible in any field.

Lauryn's ability to switch between sports highlights the importance of being open to change and new opportunities. She excelled in both sprinting and bobsledding, showing that versatility can lead to amazing achievements. Lauryn's story encourages us to be adaptable and willing to explore new paths. By embracing change and being open to new experiences, we can discover our full potential and achieve success in diverse areas.

Her achievements in both individual and team sports emphasize the power of collaboration and teamwork. While she shined as a sprinter, her success in bobsledding required close cooperation with her teammates. Lauryn's story teaches us that working together and supporting one another can lead to greater accomplishments. By valuing teamwork and building strong partnerships, we can reach our goals more effectively and enjoy the journey together.

Finally, her social advocacy inspires us to use our talents and platforms to create positive change in our communities. Beyond her athletic achievements, Lauryn has dedicated herself to helping others and promoting social causes. Her story encourages us to leverage our skills and success to make a meaningful impact. By giving back and standing up for what we believe in, we can contribute to a better world and inspire others to do the same.

LAURYN WILLIAMS FUN FACTS

- Throughout her career, Lauryn secured multiple medals at the World Championships in Athletics. She won two gold medals in Helsinki in 2005 and another gold and a silver in Osaka in 2007.

- Education is really important to Lauryn. She earned a bachelor's degree in finance from the University of Miami in 2004 and continued her education while training for the 2008 Olympics. She then went on to receive a master's in business administration from the University of Phoenix in 2009.

THINGS TO THINK ABOUT

- Lauryn excelled in both track and bobsledding. Who supports you in your endeavors, and how can you be a team player like Lauryn?
- Lauryn showed versatility by competing in different sports. What other talents do you have, and how can you explore them just like Lauryn did?
- What do you think Lauryn's mindset was like during tough races, and how can you adopt a winning mindset in your challenges?

TO SUM THINGS UP

From the starting blocks to the frosty bobsled tracks, Lauryn Williams has taken us on a thrill ride of Olympic excellence! Her journey from sprinting to sliding is like a whirlwind adventure, showing us that anything is possible with grit and versatility.

Now, it's time to wrap up and ponder upon all the exciting and inspiring stories and achievements we've learned about. Who knows, maybe one of you will be the next to inspire others, so grab your gear and get ready to blaze your own trail in the exhilarating race toward your dreams!

BEFORE YOU GO...

Feeling inspired? Then take a moment to share that inspiration with someone else!

Simply by sharing your honest opinion of this book and a little about what you found here, you'll continue the work of these incredible athletes and spread the inspiration they have to share far and wide.

LET'S HEAR FROM YOU!

Thank you so much for your support. Remember: No matter what happens, hold onto your dreams and do what it takes to achieve them.

Scan the QR code below

CONCLUSION

As we turn the final page of this inspiring collection, let's take a moment to reflect on the incredible journeys of the Olympians we've met. Each athlete's story shows us the power of the human spirit, teaching us invaluable lessons about perseverance, resilience, and self-belief. These stories aren't just about winning medals; they're about overcoming obstacles, breaking barriers, and making a lasting impact on the world.

From Michael Phelps' relentless dedication to swimming, earning him 28 Olympic medals, to Wilma Rudolph's journey from being unable to walk to becoming the fastest woman in the world, we've learned that perseverance and hard work are key to achieving our goals.

Simone Biles and Usain Bolt exemplify the importance of embracing our uniqueness and using it as a strength. Simone's story of overcoming early childhood challenges and becoming the greatest gymnast of all time shows us that our unique qualities are what make us powerful.

Meanwhile, Usain Bolt's path to Olympic greatness, from running in a small town in Jamaica to becoming the fastest man on Earth shows us that believing in our abilities and embracing our differences really can lead to extraordinary success.

April Ross and Alix Klineman's ability to adapt to new challenges and environments in their sport teaches us the importance of being flexible and open to change. Similarly, Lauryn Williams's success in both sprinting and bobsledding highlights the value of versatility. Their stories encourage us to explore different interests and adapt to new situations, proving that flexibility can lead to amazing achievements.

Nathan Chen and Nadia Comaneci's stories remind us of the power of mental strength and focus. Nathan's ability to balance his academic pursuits with his figure skating career teaches us the importance of finding balance in our lives. Nadia's unwavering focus during her gymnastics routines, leading to perfect 10s, shows us that remaining focused on our goals is crucial for success.

Bonnie Blair and Carl Lewis's stories highlight the importance of having a strong support system and the power of teamwork. Bonnie's success in speed skating was supported by her coaches and teammates, emphasizing the value of surrounding ourselves with people who believe in us. Carl's achievements in both individual and relay events showcase the power of collaboration and the importance of supporting each other to reach common goals.

Muhammad Ali and Jesse Owens both used their platforms to advocate for social justice and equality. Ali's bold stance against racial discrimination and Owens' defiance of Nazi ideology at the 1936 Berlin Olympics remind us of the impact we can have when we stand up for what is right. Their stories inspire us to use our talents and voices to make a positive difference in the world.

Meanwhile, Marit Bjørgen and Shaun White remind us to dream big and stay humble. Marit's numerous Olympic wins in cross-country skiing demonstrate the power of setting lofty goals and working hard to achieve them. Shaun White's journey from a young snowboarder to a legend in winter sports teaches us the importance of staying true to ourselves and being proud of our achievements while remaining grounded.

These Olympians' stories are just the beginning. They serve as a starting point for your own journey of discovery and inspiration. Learn more about these incredible athletes and countless others who have made their mark on the Olympic stage. Let their experiences fuel your passion and drive your ambitions.

Take the winning spirit of these Olympians and bring it on your journey. Gear up and get ready to conquer your dreams with the same gusto. The world is your arena—it's time to make some epic plays.

If you enjoyed these stories, please consider asking your parents to leave a review. Your feedback helps others discover the inspiration within these pages. Now, go forth and chase your dreams. The next great sports story in the Olympic arena could be yours to have! Claim all the glory you deserve!

REFERENCES

Abel, S. (2023, October 30). *8 captivating facts about Katarina Witt*. Facts.net. https://facts.net/celebrity/8-captivating-facts-about-katarina-witt/

Ali, M. (2019). *Muhammad Ali quotes*. BrainyQuote. https://www.brainyquote.com/authors/muhammad-ali-quotes

Alix Klineman. (n.d.). USA Volleyball. https://usavolleyball.org/athlete/alix-klineman/

Alix Klineman. (2024, April 19). Wikipedia. https://en.wikipedia.org/w/index.php?title=Alix_Klineman&oldid=1219713698

April Ross. (n.d.). USA Volleyball. https://usavolleyball.org/athlete/april-ross/

April Ross. (2024, May 15). Wikipedia. https://en.wikipedia.org/w/index.php?title=April_Ross&oldid=1224023526

Augustyn, A. (2018). Jesse Owens | biography & facts. In *Encyclopædia Britannica*. https://www.britannica.com/biography/Jesse-Owens

Augustyn, A. (2020). Katie Ledecky | American swimmer. In *Encyclopædia Britannica*. https://www.britannica.com/biography/Katie-Ledecky

Bazilchuk, N. (2018, February 22). *How to train like the world's most successful female cross-country skier*. Norwegian SciTech News. https://norwegianscitechnews.com/2018/02/train-like-worlds-successful-female-cross-country-skier/

Biles, S. (n.d.). *Simone Biles quotes*. BrainyQuote. https://www.brainyquote.com/authors/simone-biles-quotes

Biradar, V. (2016, August 16). *10 Interesting facts about Usain Bolt*. Spyn. https://spyn.co/blog/interesting-facts-about-usain-bolt/

Bjorgen, M. (n.d.). *Marit Bjorgen quotes*. BrainyQuote. https://www.brainyquote.com/authors/marit-bjorgen-quotes

Bolt, U. (n.d.). *Usain Bolt quotes*. BrainyQuote. https://www.brainyquote.com/authors/usain-bolt-quotes

Bonnie Blair. (n.d.-a). Encyclopedia Britannica. https://www.britannica.com/biography/Bonnie-Blair

Bonnie Blair. (n.d.-b). Britannica Kids. https://kids.britannica.com/students/article/Bonnie-Blair/310258

Bonnie Blair. (n.d.-c). Encyclopedia Britannica. https://www.britannica.com/biography/Bonnie-Blair

Bonnie Blair. (2020, September 18). Olympics. https://olympics.com/en/athletes/bonnie-blair

Bonnie Blair. (2024, May 8). Wikipedia. https://en.wikipedia.org/w/index.php?title=Bonnie_Blair&oldid=1222877806

Bonnie Blair quotes. (n.d.). BrainyQuote. https://www.brainyquote.com/authors/bonnie-blair-quotes

Brothers, M. (2023, October 24). *10 surprising facts about Nadia Comaneci.* Facts.net. https://facts.net/celebrity/10-surprising-facts-about-nadia-comaneci/

Burack, E. (2021, June 22). *18 things to know about Alix Klineman, the Jewish beach volleyball star.* Hey Alma. https://www.heyalma.com/18-things-to-know-about-alix-klineman-the-jewish-beach-volleyball-star/

Buzinski, J. (2021, July 28). *Figure skater Nathan Chen apologizes for homophobic remarks.* OutSports. https://www.outsports.com/2021/7/28/22597517/nathan-chen-homophobic-figure-skater-remarks-apology/

Callahan, S. (2022, June 13). *10 facts about Muhammad Ali.* History Hit. https://www.historyhit.com/facts-about-muhammad-ali/

Carl Lewis. (2019, July 20). United States Olympic & Paralympic Museum. https://usopm.org/carl-lewis/

Carl Lewis. (n.d.). Food and Agriculture Organization of the United Nations. https://www.fao.org/yunga/background/ambassadors/carl-lewis/en/

Chen, N. (n.d.). *Nathan Chen Quotes.* BrainyQuote. https://www.brainyquote.com/authors/nathan-chen-quotes

Chloe Kim. (n.d.). Encyclopaedia Britannica. https://www.britannica.com/biography/Chloe-Kim

Chloe Kim biography, Olympic medals, records and age. (n.d.). Olympics. https://olympics.com/en/athletes/chloe-kim

Chloe Kim quotes. (n.d.). BrainyQuote. https://www.brainyquote.com/authors/chloe-kim-quotes

Cogswell, M. (2023, August 19). *34 facts about Shaun White.* Facts.net. https://facts.net/celebrity/34-facts-about-shaun-white/

DiGiacomo, P. (2018). Kim Yuna | South Korean figure skater. In *Encyclopædia Britannica.* https://www.britannica.com/biography/Kim-Yu-Na

Dowd, K. E. (2017, April 28). *Michael Phelps opens up about ADHD struggles.* Sports Illustrated. https://www.si.com/olympics/2017/04/28/michael-phelps-opens-about-adhd-struggles-teacher-told-me-id-never-amount-anything

The Editors of Encyclopaedia Britannica. (n.d.). *Carl Lewis.* Encyclopedia Britannica. https://www.britannica.com/biography/Carl-Lewis

The Editors of Encyclopedia Britannica. (2018). Michael Phelps. In *Encyclopædia Britannica.* https://www.britannica.com/biography/Michael-Phelps

The Editors of Encyclopedia Britannica. (2019). Nadia Comaneci. In *Encyclopædia Britannica.* https://www.britannica.com/biography/Nadia-Comaneci

Eric Heiden. (n.d.). Encyclopaedia Brittanica. https://www.britannica.com/biography/Eric-Heiden

Eric Heiden. (2020, September 18). Olympics. https://olympics.com/en/athletes/eric-heiden

Eric Heiden | American athlete. (n.d.). Encyclopedia Britannica. https://www.britannica.com/biography/Eric-Heiden

Escobar, S. (2016, August 11). *13 fun facts that will make you love Simone Biles even more.* Good Housekeeping. https://www.goodhousekeeping.com/life/inspirational-stories/news/g3779/who-is-simone-biles/

44 facts about Michael Phelps. (2023, August 19). Facts.net. https://facts.net/celebrity/44-facts-about-michael-phelps/

48 facts about Simone Biles. (2023, August 19). Facts.net. https://facts.net/celebrity/48-facts-about-simone-biles/

Furman, T. (2006, October 22). *Eric Heiden facts.* Tom Furman Fitness. https://www.tomfurman.com/eric-heiden-facts/

Furr, F. (2023, October 30). *25 mind-blowing facts about Yuna Kim.* Facts.net. https://facts.net/celebrity/25-mind-blowing-facts-about-yuna-kim/

Gay, C. (2023, May 25). *87 years ago, Jesse Owens set five world records in 45 minutes as Ohio State sprinter.* The Columbus Dispatch. https://www.dispatch.com/story/sports/college/track-field/2023/05/25/jesse-owens-world-records-ohio-state-track-big-ten-championships-87-years/70251927007/

Gunston, J. (2023, October 8). *Simone Biles: All titles, records and medals - complete list.* Olympics. https://olympics.com/en/news/simone-biles-all-titles-records-medals-complete-list

Harness, N. (2023, November 9). *16 unbelievable facts about April Ross.* Facts.net. https://facts.net/celebrity/16-unbelievable-facts-about-april-ross/

Hauser, T. (2018). Muhammad Ali. In *Encyclopædia Britannica.* https://www.britannica.com/biography/Muhammad-Ali-boxer

Heiden, E. (n.d.). *Eric Heiden quote: "It is not the events in our life that define our character, but how we deal with them."* QuoteFancy. https://quotefancy.com/quote/1746362/Eric-Heiden-It-is-not-the-events-in-our-life-that-define-our-character-but-how-we-deal

IOC. (2016). *Paavo Nurmi biography, Olympic medals, records and age.* Olympics. https://olympics.com/en/athletes/paavo-nurmi

Jesse Owens. (2024, May 10). Wikipedia. https://en.wikipedia.org/w/index.php?title=Jesse_Owens&oldid=1223193476

Jester, B. (2023, October 24). *15 surprising facts about Carl Lewis.* Facts.net. https://facts.net/celebrity/15-surprising-facts-about-carl-lewis/

Katarina Witt. (n.d.-a). Encyclopedia Britannica. https://www.britannica.com/biography/Katarina-Witt

Katarina Witt. (n.d.-b). Olympics. https://olympics.com/en/athletes/katarina-witt

Katie Ledecky biography, Olympic medals, records and age. (n.d.). Olympics. https://olympics.com/en/athletes/katie-ledecky

Kim Yuna. (2020, September 18). Olympics. https://olympics.com/en/athletes/yuna-kim

Kim Yuna quotes. (n.d.). BrainyQuote. https://www.brainyquote.com/authors/kim-yuna-quotes

Klein, C. (2018, August 30). *10 things you may not know about Jesse Owens.* History. https://www.history.com/news/10-things-you-may-not-know-about-jesse-owens

Lauryn Williams. (n.d.). Olympics. https://olympics.com/en/athletes/lauryn-williams

Lauryn Williams. (n.d.). TVGuide. https://www.tvguide.com/celebrities/lauryn-williams/bio/3000385281/

Ledecky, K. (n.d.). *Katie Ledecky quotes.* BrainyQuote. https://www.brainyquote.com/authors/katie-ledecky-quotes

Lewis, C. (n.d.). *Carl Lewis quotes.* BrainyQuote. https://www.brainyquote.com/authors/carl-lewis-quotes

Lindstrom, S. (2019). Usain Bolt | biography, medals, & facts. In *Encyclopædia Britannica.* https://www.britannica.com/biography/Usain-Bolt

List of career achievements by Nathan Chen. (2024, May 3). Wikipedia. https://en.wikipedia.org/w/index.php?title=List_of_career_achievements_by_Nathan_Chen&oldid=1221992245

Luan Peszek. (2019). Simone Biles | biography, medals, & facts. In *Encyclopædia Britannica.* https://www.britannica.com/biography/Simone-Biles

Makin, K. (2022, April 29). "My conscience won't let me": What Muhammad Ali teaches us today. *Christian Science Monitor.* https://www.csmonitor.com/Commentary/2022/0429/My-conscience-won-t-let-me-What-Muhammad-Ali-teaches-us-today

Marit Bjoergen. (n.d.). Encyclopaedia Brittanica. https://www.britannica.com/biography/Marit-Bjorgen

Marit Bjørgen. (2024, May 20). Wikipedia. https://en.wikipedia.org/w/index.php?title=Marit_Bj%C3%B8rgen&oldid=1224742093

Mead, W. (2022, September 9). *Simone Biles - age, brother & gymnastics.* Biography. https://www.biography.com/athletes/simone-biles

Michael Phelps: "Don't be afraid to dream as big as you possibly can." (2021, July 31). Olympics. https://olympics.com/en/news/michael-phelps-don-t-be-afraid-to-dream-as-big-as-you-possibly-can

Mosier, R. (2023, October 10). *19 unbelievable facts about Chloe Kim.* Facts.net. https://facts.net/celebrity/19-unbelievable-facts-about-chloe-kim/

Nadia Comaneci biography, Olympic medals, records and age. (n.d.). Olympics. https:// olympics.com/en/athletes/nadia-comaneci

Nadia Comaneci quotes. (n.d.). BrainyQuote. https://www.brainyquote.com/authors/nadia-comaneci-quotes

Nathan Chen. (n.d.). Britannica Kids. https://kids.britannica.com/students/article/Nathan-Chen/634138

Nathan Chen. (2022, July 29). Team USA. https://www.teamusa.com/profiles/nathan-chen-866079

Norwood, A. (2017). *Wilma Rudolph.* DEV: National Women's History Museum. https:// www.womenshistory.org/education-resources/biographies/wilma-rudolph

Olympic legend Bjoergen reveals the secrets behind her record-breaking career. (2020, March 21). Olympics. https://olympics.com/en/news/olympic-legend-bjoergen-reveals-the-secrets-behind-her-record-breaking-career

Owens, J. (2019). *Jesse Owens quotes.* BrainyQuote. https://www.brainyquote. com/authors/jesse-owens-quotes

Paavo Nurmi | Finnish athlete. (n.d.). Encyclopedia Britannica. https://www. britannica.com/biography/Paavo-Nurmi

Phelps, M. (n.d.). *71 Michael Phelps Quotes.* BrainyQuote. https://www. brainyquote.com/authors/michael-phelps-quotes

Piccotti, T. (2021, October 22). *Muhammad Ali.* Biography. https://www. biography.com/athletes/muhammad-ali

Rudolph, W. (2019). *Wilma Rudolph quotes.* BrainyQuote. https://www. brainyquote.com/authors/wilma-rudolph-quotes

Sack, M. (2023, October 28). *23 intriguing facts about Katie Ledecky.* Facts.net. https://facts.net/celebrity/23-intriguing-facts-about-katie-ledecky/

Sakavitsi, K. (2024, January 11). *The History of the Olympic Games.* Olympics. https://olympics.com/en/news/the-history-of-the-olympic-games

Shapiro, E. (2023, October 13). *15 mind-blowing facts about Usain Bolt.* Facts. net. https://facts.net/celebrity/15-mind-blowing-facts-about-usain-bolt/

Shaun White. (n.d.). Team USA. https://www.teamusa.com/profiles/shaun-white

Shaun White. (2018, February 15). Biography. https://www.biography.com/ athlete/shaun-white

Shaun White | American athlete. (2020). In *Encyclopædia Britannica.* https:// www.britannica.com/biography/Shaun-White

10 fast facts about Wilma Rudolph. (2020, August 4). MentalFloss. https://www. mentalfloss.com/article/627123/wilma-rudolph-facts

10 things to know about Olympian Lauryn Williams. (n.d.). BET. https://www.bet. com/photo-gallery/2dzkso/10-things-to-know-about-olympian-lauryn-williams/zlnfe7

30 best Paavo Nurmi quotes with image. (n.d.). Bookey. https://www.bookey.app/ quote-author/paavo-nurmi

Top 100 Shaun White quotes (2024 Update). (n.d.). QuoteFancy. https:// quotefancy.com/shaun-white-quotes

The unifying power of the Olympic Games to bring the world together in peaceful competition - Olympic News. (2021, July 15). Olympics. https://olympics. com/ioc/news/the-unifying-power-of-the-olympic-games-to-bring-the-world-together-in-peaceful-competition

Usain Bolt. (2024, May 19). Wikipedia. https://en.wikipedia.org/w/index. php?title=Usain_Bolt&oldid=1224607547

Usain Bolt, the fastest man in the world has scoliosis. (2015, March 9). Spiral Spine. https://spiralspine.com/usain-bolt-fastest-man-has-scoliosis/

Weaver, E. (2018, January 4). *9 things you didn't know about figure skater Nathan Chen, including his pre-routine ritual.* Popsugar. https://www.popsugar. com/fitness/who-nathan-chen-44470534

Whiteman, H. (2016, June 4). *"Sting like a bee": Best quotes from Muhammad Ali.* CNN. https://www.cnn.com/2016/06/04/sport/best-quotes-muhammad-ali/index.html

Who I am. (n.d.). Lauryn Williams. https://www.lauryn-williams.com/meet-lauryn

Wilder, C. (2016, August 16). *15 moments (so far) that have made these Olympics so fun to watch.* For the Win. https://ftw.usatoday.com/2016/08/15-best-moments-rio-olympics-usain-bolt-michael-phelps-simone-biles

Williams, L. (n.d.). *Quotes by Lauryn Williams.* A-Z Quotes. https://www. azquotes.com/author/44361-Lauryn_Williams

Wilma Rudolph | American athlete. (2018). In *Encyclopædia Britannica.* https:// www.britannica.com/biography/Wilma-Rudolph

Witt, K. (n.d.). *Katarina Witt quotes.* BrainyQuote. https://www.brainyquote. com/authors/katarina-witt-quotes

Woodin, A. (2024, March 15). *Olympic sprinter Usain Bolt is inspiring a new generation of athletes: "Anything is possible."* NBC Insider Official Site. https://www.nbc.com/nbc-insider/olympics-sprinter-usain-bolt-now-record-medals-height

Made in the USA
Las Vegas, NV
04 July 2024

91844117R00089